What is the inside, what is outside?

Edited by Leslie Scalapino

O / two An Anthology

O BOOKS :: OAKLAND 1991

Carla Harryman / Leslie Scalapino / Fanny Howe
Laura Moriarty / Lynne Dreyer / Alan Davies / Gil Ott
Mei-mei Berssenbrugge / Richard Tuttle / Kit Robinson
Cydney Chadwick / Karen Kelly / Geoffrey O'Brien
Bernadette Mayer / Clark Coolidge
Victor Hernández Cruz / Anne Waldman / Bruce Andrews
Aaron Shurin / Laura Feldman / Norma Cole
Tina Darragh / Harryette Mullen / Rae Armantrout
Hannah Weiner / Dennis Phillips / Todd Baron
Suzi Roberts / Beverly Dahlen / Sally Doyle
Jessica Grim / Steven Benson

TYPOGRAPHY BY GEORGE MATTINGLY DESIGN, BERKELEY.
COVER DESIGN AND PHOTO BY LESLIE SCALAPINO.

ACKNOWLEDGMENTS:
Mei-mei Berssenbrugge's poem "Hiddenness" was published in *Pequod*.

CARLA HARRYMAN

FROM: **THE WORDS**
CHAPTER 3

A child touches a flower.

Then a tip of air moves to fill the space moving a leg apart from a leg. Slightly apart, the legs will promise a little breeze to the part. A seamless song stays the tip of an invective against the child's mother. One can't see the mirror on the tip of a flower.

> The cool child is father to the man
> The hard child is mother to the man
> The quiet child is mother to the woman
> The burning child is father to the woman

is sung and the singing goes on while the mother arranges a bouquet with irritation. Even so, this mother would make a better congress person than the X man. This is written on one of the spools All-the-Loss-That-Ever-Was one day dropped off at the museum where there had been a group of pressmen and presswomen dropping in on Boltanski.

In defiance of the mother's flower estate, the legs part a little farther in the song, and the mother's body's gold mountainside and baby pragmatism collide. You can not, says the strange doctrine, written with this mother's clash.

But defeat will be remade into rapture.

Or myriad seeds when struck by passing war machines will give birth to comedy.

Is that so, thinks the Chair, or the nihilist, the Romanticized-Hell-Grabbers, or even the man lurking around the magazines at the drugstore when they encounter such slogans. Is it so that defeat will be remade into rapture, or that machines will give birth to comedy, or that

3

one can not when a mother says it, they think with the same thought as if all of them were the same person.

It was so that a chair was a chair in a room. Shadows curved in the room. A warm blue flew up our backs in the morning when morning was a seam stitched up by birds. Night had fallen into an abandoned trough halfway down the dune over which the nihilist traveled in his incubus by day and by night. Sometimes we would speculate from our bed that he was bolted down by blankets and that's why he could speak freely on any subject. We were convinced that his claims became our own thoughts, and we would lay in bed thinking this and other things such as a machine is superior to a prop. Parroting the nihilist's formula (there is a standard of measurement and value for anything, since there are as many possible standards of measurement and value as there are combinations of things in words) I would name all the things that were superior and what they were superior to.

The word glove is superior to the object glove. A hand is superior to a glove. A puppet glove is superior to a puppet hand. A puppet is superior to a doll. A doll is superior to a combat unit. A soldier in a combat unit is superior to a combat unit. A uniform is inferior to doll clothes. A tray is as low as a floor. But a floor is vastly superior to stockings. And then there is an assemblage of track records, which fall to the bottom of this verticality, though they're buoyed up by a hardy variety of sewing spools.

Above the secular slide and gauzy strip we see through even babies know it is not possible to read someone's mind. The slip shutter of pressmen and presswomen reaching for dots of Boltanski's thinking to turn into ink is as innocent as reading someone's mind, in spite of the spools of words floating overhead that contradict speech by turning it into objects. Boltanski says there is a dead child in each of us and the newspaper says it tomorrow. Flying babies write on spools floating above the exhibition's landscape as if they themselves were an exhibit of daydreams and what they write are the missing words that predate an artist's epiphany.

Word-laden spools exit from the museum and float over our village contradicting newsworthy statements. There is a joke that they pollute the pollution as they bounce through the ozone brought in by the city wind. Watch out has never been reported in the newspaper to have been seen dancing on a dancing spool in the sky, but when we read, we imagine the pressperson writing down words ejaculated from the frought and frozen voices of a world as if they were the observations of a fully neutral interlocutor and we say watch out.

When we get serious like this, the nihilist laughs at us and this is why: his demon is his mode of transportation. The "Hello" painted in gold on his liver from the time of his birth was a gift from the doctor alias the father, a joker with a child living inside him. (The doctor father likes to refer to himself variously as the house of chores, the heap of sighs, and sometimes even The Great Mother). The "Hello" was a baby of sorts inside a baby, of sorts. It jumped and made the little nihilist jump for joy. Its tongue could reach his heart and his heart rolled him up and tumbled him one eve all fleecy down the hills to the swamp where the chill and shine around the misting trees opened its appetite to the Romanticized-Hell-Grabbers, who were holding a union meeting about their current unemployment. But the baby nihilist did not know what it meant to be serious. His heart jumped with fleece and shine when the "Hello" inside him licked it.

There was nothing that did not permit everybody to be in the same place at one time so everybody even those in magenta hats and buttoned suits and those of us smitten by slow sex and those of us who turned around about each other with such abandon that we thought we turned around inside each other and those of us who took notes for the newspaper and the magazine sellers and the photo of one child with the magic fatal worldly eyes, even the creep looking at the photo in front of the aspirin display, the relatives and clowns, the fidgeter and the struggler, a woman eating didactic wall-hangings at the underground market, All Done, One Chair and the Billboard Baby, All-the-Loss-That-Ever-Was, the mother fish, the scientist, and the Daily's parading their reliquaries visited the swamp on that misty moon lit eve with chill and shine hanging around the trees like open appetites. Of course, there were those of us who bunched up and popped from contagious glee when the "Hello" licked the heart of the baby nihilist and there were those of us who respected the quiet of a meeting. Words said we could do this or even something else. But none of us had a word written in us at birth except the baby nihilist which is what makes his grown body lonely, his tongue a flame, and his mode of transportation a demon.

His is no doubt a slicker portrait than you could have wished; though tomorrow, if someone points to the heart and says, "I feel it right here," think twice about the meaning if you want to be serious.

Now, in daylight the spool babies will de-slick the portraits with their untreated words that pollute the ozone when it blows in from the city and that is why, when it is polluted, comedy, which blooms out of the sky's largesse, will be blue smashed to mustard on the back of our shirts. A parade of beetles will cross the road like skeletons in a line and follow All Done to the edge of a looming factory's shadow where one can sit peacefully and listen to water. The skeletons will jerk in and out of culture. Names will call out after us. "And X! X equals a perfectly virtuous person." The spool babies will tell us we are not that person. They will know it is not possible to read someone's mind. People often think the same thoughts to different effect is exactly what the spool babies will write in our thoughts.

A doll is superior to a combat unit.

Some of us wonder who speaks. But one can't see the mirror on the tip of a flower.

In the cool of the night the jury speaks out of turn so we dream it while peddling backwards. It says everybody who has slept and everybody who has no place to sleep wants the beneficial light of day. The rest of its opinion is summed up thusly:

1). He's got and he doesn't have. There is and there isn't enough. We wanted to know where she was. He shared and ate onions. It was raining in the early morning and wet. His jacket zipper was broken and this made him chillier. Therefore, the cool child is father to the man.

2). It is not easy to fondle oneself sexually in front of 15 other homeless refugees standing in front of a fire in the city park. It is also difficult to have autoerotic fantasies in front of one's mother. Therefore, the hard child is mother to the man.

3). The girl becomes her mother when the wind flies into her open legs. Therefore, the quiet child is mother to the woman.

4). In the soup kitchen, he hears his words lying before he speaks so he keeps his mouth shut in order not to be severed from his breakfast. Therefore, the burning child is father to the woman.

When the newspaper said there is no story here, the spool babies wrote on their spools "there is no story here" and when the town woke up "there is no story here" was dancing across the sky.

CHAPTER 5

One day the nihilist held forth at the lily slump in the following manner:

A baroque and careful man behind the scraggly tail here, surrounded by eloquence that appears as mud to the untrained eye. Check your eye, first. Then observe the lacquered spittle at the end of the scales of the tail. Its patina resembles scorch. It is unreal scorch. Why not travel with such beauty? Why not subscribe to its tautology? I have such lessons to withhold that I have devised an entire estate for them. Every time a new lesson comes to mind I deemphasize its value by escorting it to my estate. Born within the frame of this incubus, it is discharged through the mouth. Today I have a lesson to discharge. Here we are now, CLUB DAILY. Such an estate as many have dreamed and entered. There in the darkest corner is a table of inadvertent males. The lesson is cast toward them. They take it, the lesson, to be a girl in the throws of emancipation. Outside something sweet dissolves in the noonday sun. That is the image of myself uniting with the horizon.

Now they are unsure about the girl. Perhaps it is, yes indeed it is, an acid. Chemical warfare has entered the premises. It is rather frightening. Steam from the beef stew at the table impairs their faces. To fend off danger, they discuss the advantages and disadvantages of chemical warfare while encouraging each others' appetites. "I always come here for stew." They are getting drowsy over their concerns. "It is impossible to generalize. The lesson is beginning to work. "One must generalize," another says in fierce contention with the prior statement.

We are now off and running skittering and scamping about the length of the horizon. Have you ever felt the effect of such a powerful line? A line drawn with the mind on itself? My advantage makes me a target of envy among children.

The acid, which they have feared, each secretly, would eat into the stomach, then a neck, has been tamed. The lesson is neither a girl, emancipated, flirting with dissipation in male surrounds, nor is it an outside threat. Their stomachs are warm and the lesson dreams the men in the following manner:

They come from me, the mother. Each is perfect. There are five beds on the moon. They pick up their telescopes. One estimates the size of mountains and the depth of oceans. Another sizes up civilization and makes astute observations about human groups and the relationship of agrarian to urban life and habits. Another studies weather patterns and animal behavior in respect to the weather patterns. Another observes death and writes down his observations. And one watches the watchers and watches what they watch. There are five beds and five boys and five disciplines.

After the lesson wakes up, the commissioner of the banquet hall presents our feasting boys with a trophy for their work.

CHAPTER 7

One day when everything was perfect and we were stomping on nut-shells while shucking nuts on the border between Watchout and us, we saw at the very edge of the nutshell terrain, a woman holding a child, speaking and singing in a speaking singing voice. Or sometimes she was speaking and sometimes singing. Her voice going in and out of one thing and another.

Now the edge of the nutshell terrain is a peculiar place to sit alone with a child you are singing and talking to at the same time. Singing and talking at the edge of the nutshell terrain reminds me of sitting in the water at the very edge of a big pool of water where small fish rile up spinnets of mud and the mud coats you turning your legs into nylon-stocking-coated legs that are really mud-coated legs. It also reminds me of something else, something a little bit sad and a little bit hot and bright at the same time. The sun stings your feet there a little more than it stings them someplace else. The light dissipates your energy there more than it dissipates energy someplace else. The tree on the edge is less of a tree than a tree someplace else. It takes the blows of heat, light, and wind before any excess of heat, light, and wind reaches its fellow trees in the center of the nutshell terrain where everything can be perfect, the way it was on the day we were stomping nutshells and shucking nuts.

So there was the talking singing woman under the tree with a child in her lap. This is what I recall she said; although, I don't know if we would all agree these were her words, because we never discussed these words among ourselves after:

"They put away their moon machines and latched onto me, they put away their doll gunnies, their strike carriers, their nest pills with the oil traveling through the center of desert sweepers, they put away their sting nozzles and bruisers, they put away their lip machines with the bullet proof words that defend them against lip machines with bullet proof words from somewhere else. And they latched onto me, just the way you do sometimes," she said to her child while singing to the child at the same time.

"They said they would do this before they did it. They called me up. They even called me when there was nobody to call and only one thing to think about. They called me from the heart of a desert sweeper. The sweeper's grunts from the heart of the desert were so angry that the children's voices were empty pie shells. No names, no identities, no songs, just empty pie shells calling me up because they said they came from me as if I were a town or a house or something bigger than a town or a house. "This" she said, looking at the child now sleeping on her lap, "is not a parody. It is what really happened to me; although someday, what really happened may seem very much like a parody.

"Each of these children, who seem grown but who are not, not now, who were grown yesterday, or a minute ago, but not now, fell on me as if I were a blue cloud at the base of a valley of blankets. So I made up their room and placed each child in a bed in the room, which was as long and narrow as the Straight of Magellan. Each child in each bed surmised that he or she had a mother, who, like me, is only half real, or half whole, since the mother's body is without limit to the child's wishes. A child's wishes makes a mother's body part of the world of wishes. All wishes ever wished arrive one at a time. There is a mother for each of us each child dreams dreaming also that he or she is right.

"When I stood as a guard over the beds while they slept, I noticed the glow from a moon machine belching under a pillow, I spied the stipple from a doll gunnie chipped on the floor under a bed and the remains of a bullet proof letter resting on a bedpost. But when I looked out the window, I saw between the flat dark trees two galaxies to the South of our galaxy, watching and waiting without limit."

CHAPTER 8

FOR MELISSA RILEY

At the top of the great heap, the heap of men with its unimaginable joinings of electromagnetic impulses, they lounge at appropriately luxurious distances from each other. Every once in a while, one of them moves in, pressing his supple body forward toward the others in order to impress upon them his personal 10th century aura of disappointment— in a woman, her jealousy, her compensatory behavior, her vain efforts to keep her flaws regulated invisibly in her own internal stream of self knowledge, a knowledge she adroitly makes much of while under the delusion that she can successfully conceal one or more than one personal weakness. Sadly, he has noticed that she has dwelled too much on one or another personal weakness, seeing it as she has, from her flawed imagining of the man's view

from where there would be no negative memories to live with if he were married to the perfect woman. " The ideal does not exist," remarks one of his cohorts. A shutter shakes the rectilinear habitation of the group. For one second, swarms of male energy from under the heap have the urge to give way. A jelly-like tremble under the habitation occurs, men's bodies in the forms of

> rivulet
> with rivulet
> anything
> could be hinged
> or subordinate

rocks, earth, mulch, arms in the forms of elegantly planed boards, torsos curved permanently into the shape of entranceways all shake simultaneously. After this only vaguely noticeable convulsion, the heap resumes, what was never truly parted from, its previously predetermined position, ten centuries later, dreaming the elaborate male population, still. And all is presently still. In front, a sluggish sky halos a diminishing light, and behind, a blue as serious as a working woman's slate shirt blasts Watchout with its suspiciously ethical, doctrinaire, overintellectualized pro-choice hue. Above us, the spool babies float by displaying their word laden spools that say things like: "make believe is nurtured by suspicion," "parody is the bastion of authority," "discussion braced by inhibition provokes a ripe imagination"

in kids books, the ones we inhale from time to time by the gas pumps in the attendant's little round library. After an hour's nauseatingly disciplined read, we write over the words with our own sticky fungus words, or sometimes we use the ripe cotillion words that slip down from our suspiciously ethical, doctrinaire, overintellectualized pro-choice dreams. This is a technique we have learned from reading headlines in the newspaper on many consecutive mornings in the wee hours before our bodies stick and roll away

into other stories across the border of Watchout where we are accompanied by our automaton, who we recently liberated from a display case in the museum labeled "Automatons March through Time." Just now a sniffling, scruffy boy scuttles down the street, stops to pee on a varnished lawn. Upon close examination, we discover that he is one of us. Then a furry looking girl tears a rag off a toy clown holding a miniature movie projector. The clown, too, is one of us. A book falls from the girl's dress as she dances on one of the garden walkways. It is ugly as a tossed out greasy paper sack left behind by the city dumpster on a Wednesday. It must be an old book, an engineering manual from 1935 perhaps, something she picked from a trash can, something in Greek or Spanish. But just like the boy and the clown, the book is ours smelling of gasoline and grime and the girl is one of us. This is what we see: that we have become wild and fearful ponies leashed into a parade, but we are not what we see. We shift down Watchout's paved drives

lead by the nihilist in his icon left over from a culture's miscellaneous bell tomes. When he sees us, he abandons his post at the top and charges toward us, greeting us with an infusion of paternal sounds. It begins to rain. He reaches into the cuff of his sleeve and pulls out a small wooden box. Inside the box is a wooden woman holding a tiny child on the border between Watchout and us. She is singing

> rivulet
> with rivulet
> hinged and subordinate

and speaking to the child at the same time. When waxing pedagogical the nihilist generally has a soporific effect on us, and this occasion proves no exception. Our automaton, cradling his broom in the middle of the street, weeps while we, the stranded, sleep.

FROM 3 PARTS OF: **WAKING LIFE**

So soldiers are cattle before. Actually. They're saying (of an event) is the source. And then as such, it is not valued by society (or believed) because it's them saying that.

And it is creating reality.

It does not cease therefore because the source occurs after. They're saying something which has occurred.

If having these sources is the same as seeing, we are free like cattle.

The event has not occurred, in a way. War has. It is not tradition, which never occurs.

So the comic book never occurs – nor is it (their) tradition. and so it is out in front.

Just a fleck like the car. Fans on stocks the car's blown by.

Coming from the dust storm, the car enters that area of the fans turning slowly on stocks on those barren hills. The car, so it's from the motor – and there's no motor there in the hills.

It doesn't repeat.

A man gets out of his car when it's 113° Fahrenheit pelted by magnolia blossoms from the Santa Ana wind.

> ghouls with pumps by their
> cars that are
> pushed out after dawn

The ghouls with pumps are like the conquered people – the one who played the harp's soldiers seen as outside and lonely, had brutalized – who're calm and gentle.

outside and lonely who'd brutalized the people – who're innocent and therefore the flesh isn't affected.

one who is in rage walks along the street
and yet others who are not as they innocent remain so

Cripples coming off van in chair unloaded onto the street their heads bobbing as grateful and apologetic – moving through them on the street going by in the morning – are not affected

though injured are in rage
they are beside it – either

and so are not affected.

That's the way they appear. One is in rage. Some with pumps at the gas station lot open and gentle – as one being also innocent is in misery that does not affect one's flesh.

It lifts that outside up, is out in front – inaccurate like feelers.

When rage affects the flesh
This is felt only later. It lifts that outside up out in front, and is mistaken for observation.

Rage is entangled thinking and neutral. It is itself pushed out after dawn and therefore useless.

That's because I don't remember being utterly sickened by it from in my cells.

but skittering across the gas station lot was in the later action of that without remembering it.

When the flesh is injured, it does not remember. So we are free like cattle.

Flesh not remembering as they're unloaded off the van in their chairs heads bobbing like flowers – and walking through them is not remembering either.

We're not there.

Walking is only remembering and so we're free like cattle.

I don't know about you but I'm a hothouse flower, someone said to me. as thrown out to make a living immediately

     that's what that is

To be a hothouse flower at the time. There isn't commentary. Outside. Alone.

I had a dream about this blasted idiot whom I'd known who I'd never want to see again with the characteristic of a child. He was in the military now in the dream coming on a cruiser in the Sudan; what was already known about his character before is simply there. in that.

He had the same idiocy of child in the dream as he had, as if one is to accept it

Having the dream is being outside, alone. Sleeping simply. The dog lying in the gutter.

The hothouse flower, the introvert, is dual.

     and so never can be in the civilization

If you say commentary, they like that but not as it is as real.

yet they like commentary, alone.

That's why there isn't that – and is dual. That characteristic in the introvert, is not valued by society just as the conquered people by the one who'd played the harp's soldiers, are not seen.

She is calm – part of her that is out in front is, though not in her cells. The part that was born is.

Alone except for the part that was born.

So fucking with the man who's like the people not the soldiers, who really are completely calm, is with the part that was born.
riding on the stem, later
is out on the street, that's a joke
who like commentary, alone
screwing who's hearing the harp rather than the soldiers and therefore completely calm –

comes

People's flesh doesn't remember because they haven't had anything to eat at the time

interpreting commentary as free
from the lovely city

This is like De Quincey's dream – anyone could have had it easily, though I didn't read it (the end, with the dream in it) because I was bored reading before I got to that part.
It wasn't special, they said to me. So anyone could have had it easily.
The fundamentalists are seeing people as just wanting to do what they want. and that cannot be.
All the constructions around appear to occur at the same time.

The ghouls with pumps alongside the cars will have appeared to move later.

They move really.

I have been indoors so long. One can only be a hermit.

I don't know what the beginning is. There is nothing there, as this is being the market.

We're supposed to be sleeping in the bunker. It's so hot at night, we're sleeping out about ten feet and apparently there's mortar. My friend is running. I call to him for help and call again but he turns away weeping, seeing me wounded.

the flesh in the day-which has been pushed out – but the next day it itself the day seems not to be there.

walking, the birds flying between one very tall tree and another – they do not meet.

One's flesh which had seemed to be, felt, as if it were infused with poison, now doesn't have anything in its cells

pushed out after sleep

the intense warping wave drinking of the flesh has left – and on its own one in the day which itself seems not to be there.

It doesn't matter if the mother doesn't remember the baby's birth or it. (One's own mother) – that couldn't possibly cause suffering, though someone is lashing in suffering.

It is paired and I couldn't get in time.

The soldier was depressed under heavy water and when he would come out days later – walking along, the birds flying above. It is inside out. He floats out from the heavy water

> as if it were the blooming trees that he sees
> for the first time when he's come out

Saw ragged man coming toward me with blanket he's laced around his neck hanging off of him who's not myself. Floating on the street toward me, who's not myself. It's inside out.

Warps of things that had occurred but moving very slowly that would surface, from the heavy water – but when he / not myself / having been indoors for days – sometimes without food, submerged depressed, not have anything in the cells then would have floated out.

Eat something drinking (juice can) standing in front of the Derby Food Store so that a rivulet runs down the chin and throat – of that is floating out. Who was inside out before that. is.

being inside out and drinking. The juice runs down the chin.

The man just getting irritated by someone in the street and opening up and just shooting them – so he is arrested, but can't tell the difference from the combat situation he's in at the same time.

there isn't a difference there – so they're like cattle

Everything is pushed out of fighting, and is mistaken for it / one's being free.

It is such a relief to know that is mistaken.

The man who's the same person out drinking juice can, the rivulet runs down the chin doesn't see the observer and so there isn't it, is standing by the Derby Food Store.

He's the source of being released

I'm him

alone

Something was set off in me later, so that not from that but visiting in another city I was cast into a rage and walked aimlessly, driven by it.

I was taken out of myself in rage, struggling. People speaking to me couldn't understand this. This was myself, in that time.

Soldier is completely free shooting. Later, he is in misery.

The woman is in her apartment who's the same person. It's a compartment. Some other man is urinating in his stall next to her wall.

the newspaper says that matronly woman is stopped on the street with boy and accused of having him as a prostitute. It is determined later that he is her son.

They value commentary, alone. And so their stopping and detaining the woman walking with her son.

Cattle just stand. Fundamentalists thrived. They're molesting a child. It is the reverse of life. Struggling like a residue when one's just wakened from before.

it is retarded in them
and so one can't understand

They create it, and that is occurring now. The child being molested, in a field.

What has created this is a mirror of them so it is not it. The mirror is empty except for them seen in it. So it is not them or it in their view. We look and don't see the observer so there isn't it.

Seeing that, it is chance.

Can't accept even that who knows more than us. Can see it.

Nor does the woman accept that jewel, who's stopped on the street and detained accused of having the boy as a prostitute who it turns out is her son.

The scrutiny in whose continuing frames this is reflected – and in which mirrors, looking for it which is occurring, it isn't seen isn't it.

and so we are free like cattle.
Alone. and knows it is and so is invalidated.

    the negative jewel
    doesn't want to

not wanting is erotic – is the time itself
    It doesn't like to be free. Weighed under in the heavy air.
    But the soldier shooting does. and in misery later.

    he is the source of being released,
    in this time

The soldier who is in misery later is this time itself.

The negative jewel has contacted the other, to do a job. He owes money
to a business. She is to pick it up, and get it to them.
    The woman meets him sitting out along the street, a crowd going by.
He is averted and so he is provocative. Inactive.
    says that he's weak. Swimming on the stem.
    She sees him, and is on the stem at the same time.
    A white disc is hanging in indigo sky, on a field on which the funda-
mentalists are molesting a child.
    The man and her are in the foreground, two speaking with the crowd
streaming by them back on their way to market.
    They're looking at really rough men who are gathered in movement
on the street.
    Green waves in which are laced dark heads. Backs in the troughs of
the green waves. Not on top of the waves.
    There are dark backs and heads laced here and there swimming in
them.
    A wave comes down.

They go by the men in the evening.

Dark corpse rolling in wave – which isn't that. head bobbing. She meets him. Trough of green waves. She is completely unsure of herself. mistaken as to others. has been. really is, has to realize that. they're dirty talking to themselves. Strolls by.

bravado is very close to complete loss of confidence

Some other attacking an older one who's unprotected – seeing herself as having been wounded by that one. Strolls by. They have each other's traits. This one (who's not her) has complete loss of confidence. Knows immature. Looks into the clearing. Mistaken has been what she was doing seeing them.

That is in reverse and light. Seeing having been mistaken who has the same traits.

They all do. There isn't a democracy, so what? That was mistaken in seeing them. That is in reverse and light also. It doesn't matter.

Figures robed in black completely covered with no eye-hole walking ahead on the dirt road – depression not being there having been before pushed out from it.

The robed little black mounds pushed out on the desert road who're walking ahead.

wave of distortion that had been there before isn't there – not of the robed black mounds figures on the road which occurs before it.

Wind blows the black robes.

The barren cliffs – walking out on them winding.

I was walking down the empty cliffs ahead of the robed with no eye-hole figures.

Who're here and there back in groups on the road.

Sheep trotting with a crazy eye on the beige-rust cliff passes me. Its senseless globular eye is floating in the mat.

Black robes blowing walk ahead on the beige-rust grass. On the rim.

A robed no eye-hole muscular movement not from it.

Blowing of the robes. Amidst the refinery.

Muscular movement not coming from one – which is from the blowing robes.

The oil fields. A refinery where no people live is on the desert. The sheep pass down to it. The crazy eye of the sheep floats in the mat as it trots.

Past.

Men moving in in tanks shooting the men of the fields who aren't living.

Seeing it only.

Censoring of duplicating as representing them. The men who aren't living and it's the market are here and there on the fields. That is atonal.

Jackknifing in the dark as a green insect. a grasshopper – weeping at night having been lying in bed, one is sitting. I thought there I hadn't been paying attention.

The soft jackknife sitting wracked in the dark. how do tears come out of the jackknifed rim? (The spliced legs and flesh are just a rim.)

The jackknife grasshopper in the dark is weeping so it is finally alert, for a minute.

Poison in the rim pushed out of the green insect in the dark afterwards.

The rim is just up to the surface of the dark. I'm a jackknifed grasshopper with soft flesh in the sense of the hopelessness of living. By that evening, I was out with him in the light neighborhood walking.

The negative jewel is in a bar and is scorned by the people there. A pouting immature woman jeers at him for not being one of them.

He's bent over, and shoots on the green velvet table.

Mumbling, they hurt him.

Man says to him cutting him who's an introvert. Outside on the lighted strip of stucco and they go in the cars.

Coming to the light. Alongside jeering at him in the dark. They tear away leaving him the cars screeching.

Meeting with him is fragile and without strain as after the grasshopper's flesh.

That's another thing, putting his mouth between the halves of the grasshopper's rim. The spliced curled legs and flesh.

This is really just for children, without there existing anything past that. But being past that.

(The hopelessness of living past that, so there is no strain) – his mouth between the grasshopper's halves in the dark.

He is languid and yet responds to their hurting him, not answering them.

Even though this is nothing as a form we support the most fascist and repressive regimes sending our military so long as this gives us wealth. This isn't fiction. It's a certain thing.

At night the negative jewel comes to the bar. He loves them.

They insist on racing playing Chicken and the man who has hurt him by jeering is killed by going over the edge. The negative jewel regrets this death and so do the others, who mourn him.

The day comes first.

The man puts his stem into the grasshopper's halves. Turning it around in it until it comes.

Cut loose in it and he is in misery from the senseless death the day coming after it. Walking in the evening. that is limpid.

The hopelessness of living is limpid in his misery.

There's a grey yellow dog lying in the gutter floating. It's sleeping. Its little red penis is extended.

Two men are walking behind the dog – the grasshopper's halves, crying, which isn't in its halves. They say he has to pay them they're running a business they say.

He has to do that. Then lying on its back. Looking at storefronts, she's walking and enters one where two men are looking at her. She says she has it and giving one of them the envelope it's revealed it isn't nearly enough. Rather than going himself, he'd sent her with it.

It's in a different part of town than where she'd gone before with it. They dump her out and then hurt on the street after taking her for a ride putting her head up against the window where people are out barely seen by them.

She's in her compartment. The man urinating in his stall next to it. Hurt.

Having been thrown on the street. And then tearing the car screeching on the street.

Weaving as it careens.

Putting the tongue to the mouth the mouth's raw, in the gutter floating.

Yellow flank is the rim, to the sky.

Then not fulfill the process.

She's moving through traffic on foot one day. Sees in the mass of scooters and cars and trucks stopped on the sheet of tin. Held at the light. Glinting on the sheet. Ahead in it is the rider who'd taken the valise. She begins walking through the mass.

It is like walking on water.

Floats on foot toward him. Who on sheet of tin whirls his neck sees her when she's back over the stalled vast expanse. Goes on moving. The fume from the motorbikes and cars pervades the air. She walks on it. Yellow teeth in neck thrashing. The motorbike pulls away then ahead on boulevard of fume.

To name it will be merely caught again in their authority as they will recognize that as themselves and one will be in their trap again.

Walk through stream of hot metal bumpers of cars that then move like plates shifting. Mass of plates and she's veering in it. On tin tail of motorbike of yellow teeth thrashing in neck. He's ahead then. On it again thrashing neck. The bike skidding and swaying in narrow channel amidst bumpers. It bucks forward. Neck bike veering and bucking out on the vast tin sheet. the sunlight is reflecting off. He wriggles free, lunging. The motorbike lunges forward. Crashes into car's side in the mass. Slippery blood on his head neck slashing. She's slashed hard slamming into car's side. Rider on foot then, veering and is way ahead then out on stalled mass.

Seeing him out on the vast reflected expanse.

The hair on the arm of a rider with a mat of blood on it. A memory of that.

She's lying in bed sprawled on the front of the nude buttocks and back, having pushed the drapery down to the ankles. The sheets are around her ankles of motorbike meeting her in mass of them.

Walks out later at night on Piazza Della Rotonda and the people are strolling. Sideways smile of men together approaching the women. There's a fountain. It's a warm night. Snorting of smoke held in their lung cage of people around the fountain.

Snorts smoke holding in his lung cage, of man in loose suit jacket, and then releases the fume. No stars can be seen in the sky.

Walking in the morning, he says that the barber is wiping his face with a towel. Heard rather than seeing an interior of room that is alongside. Then suddenly, continuing walking, facing directly into the lighted in sun room at the barber wiping his face, that is what had before been said.

She's out in one of the narrow streets alone tired walking by the hurling vehicles, in which there's no sound. One comes hurling around the corner. The rider is holding a knife, other riders moving alongside him. Cars converging in the square at the end of the street are a tin vast sheet with the riders reflected on it. She and they are reflected as are the clouds on the sheet. The rider with the knife coming for her sprawled moving reflected on the hoods, as his bike has stalled and he lunges on the hood. Above are the blue sky and the clouds which are reflected on the stalled cars so that the torsos of the riders are seen. Turning and the man hurling on the sheet. Ham the leg out hurling. A rider's head is up having been grazed. They converge with other rider who's thrown. The one with the knife continuing as she's in the maze further on. and is too far away to be reached.

There is a dark din above as if that is above the grave and not in it. This didn't occur in the square, since that was bright.

He looks at the other man as if it is terrible that you have to be bothered by that piece of fluff. They're at a dinner and the other man has had to sit down next to her. The first man expresses sympathy at him implicitly, from him having to be bothered. They sit as a group in the fume of the dinner table and talk.

A surge of people out on the narrow streets and in the squares. They're out talking and admiring each other's clothes. There's a movement of flying up inside as if in one's chest there's constriction of joy. Not like those at the dinner table. Men leaning on their motorbikes or along buildings. A thin blue evening sky with rippled clouds at the ends of the intersecting streets. The walking crowd is almost roaring.

The man in the loose suit jacket holding the fume in his lung is leaning against a building. He releases the fume of the cigarette. His black hair slicked back. Sideways smile, slouched, throwing the cigarette down moving. The crowd in front of him as on a shallow tray surging to the ends of the intersecting streets where there are squares. He steps into it.

Moving then slouched sideways-smile to her.

The crowd moving up toward slightly rippled clouds at the end of the street.

The street had been blocked off. Yet one motorbike is riding on it amidst the crowd. The rider is hugging it low, which she sees looking back. Then a memory of that rider. As she had turned forward again, but then turning her face to him. The man in the loose suit jacket has moved to where the knife makes a lunge. Hitting the bike which skids into the crowd the rider running to the end of the street.

The man in the loose suit jacket has run after him. His doing so has occurred before. Outside of her. A man in shorts someone is hurled up.

Thighs and buttocks flown shot. Hams buttocks. They converge in the blue air the muscles of the buttocks and leg rippling. A man stuck in the side is slashed.

Last night I dreamt we began to cross the parted Red Sea, B. driving unaware of the danger, T. in the back seat. The walls of the water began to come down on us. I could see them curling over us, the car surrounded and deluged. We tried the doors. We were going to drown.

Other dreams had occurred during the night. This occurs from waking life anyway. But that dream had occurred, so that's waking life.

The (other) goes to cadaver saint's apartment but on the way sees her. She's moving forward on a corner her material blowing on her. Her bags are piled behind her. She signals a cab.

Everything's waking life. Motorbikes are going by. One stalled, jump-started then its rider roaring it gunning. Others go by. The fume released from a bus which passes in front of her.

She (the other) has stepped into the street with the bus. The corner on which the woman stands is an island. The traffic hurls on either side. Might as well be the desert.

Rider comes by and sticks her. Then another as she's swept in her material. And another on the other side.

The (other) is veering amidst the motorbikes, that race on. The woman is slumped dead on the island.

The bags are gone, having been grasped by the riders. So whatever it was, the picking up of the valise was a pretence. Her being hired was to draw them away.

We're awake when we dream. Heads and bodies simply turned upside down hanging in it. The retina also.

She's sleeping and the hurling vehicles fume coming up. on it. as if on the city.

One walks; the passersby float back with the lighted weed in their hands.

They're out, motorbikes passing. They release the fume from their rib cages. Their arms float to the sides.

The sun is beating on rolls of hay under the bland sky, the fields surrounding the runway. The warp in the air is caused by something dark moving. The rest of the sky does not move. Then it is the propellers of a plane, whose body can't be seen coming in.

People running toward it so their bodies can't be seen in the light. She's running in it. Shots coming off of the side. She shoots in it. Their bodies are just flickers.

A circular wind of a tunnel from the roaring blades. They're entering the ramp. Wing off the side, of a shot.

The man in the loose suit jacket is laughing, a low sound in his rib cage, which can't be heard. Standing in the lighted tunnel the material on him flailing.

Laughing is only grinding the teeth. As the bodies have ascended.

She remembers the death of eyes lowered, sticking in the side. I have no doubts. Everything is waking life.

It is not pretending to be only the market. Or being it. Which is in reverse. Before the market.

Being the same thing but it's already been and so it's only its characteristics after, meaninglessly.

The (other) had been asleep, apprehensive. There's fear in her residual body. The heavy sleep in which she's immersed down hanging in it with the swirl around her, her eyes open, is disturbed.

Chrysalis opens, aching. Leg extended on the bed. Prone on the naked back.

She brings the rib cage up so she's sitting on the bed's edge. She's running with the bar a small person it's raining. Bike swarming. Hits the bar off the spokes of one as it's sideswiped flown. One comes by she runs on it. The bar in the spokes thrown. Man in the loose suit jacket blown on him is in between the lines of bikes. She runs on tin tail of one. He was whirling as they'd come down on him carrying knives. Bar in the spokes blown. A slash in him, running. Tin tail of one crashes swerving. They'd run. Whirling of lights on the cars.

I wonder if one could have those actions go on so there is then the thin barrier of that and oneself but not on the retina in front as everything is waking life.

I'm a hack finally, what I wanted.

They were insulting looking down on in conversation the town I'm from, and I thought it is a favorable birth. (To be from here) – to be born in a human form, seeing the others souls flitting on the periphery. In purgatory, the invention of the idea (there) of the individual illumination. It's relative.

Later on, it is. Here where mimicry doesn't mean anything.

FANNY HOWE

RANDOM AND FINITE BEING: A BIOGRAPHY

Her name was something she could stand behind. And so at first it was a word, not an image, she let herself be. As water was the beginning of zero's motion, she had a love of first sounds. Something terribly heavy though invisible hung over her early days: an interior without walls. Not small enough to avoid—still—it was like an experience (one without pain) that you dread having again.

Looking for a home NEAR home, the position of that she was always temporary. She correlated her place with the zero point, or I. Travel was a form of promiscuity she could, therefore, enjoy without guilt because little was added on. The experience of moving was more like: Get it out—beyond—a negative vowel. Each problem seemed to start at the bottom of a garden path, to say, Let's start at the bottom of this path and move up.

Her associations were like showings. You'd say "water," she'd have a vision: of waterfalls going wrong, of waves in a struggle to stay still, of slow liquid going down a drain. She built her house on water, in a sense, with the ambivalence of one who likes a confession as much as a bottle of gin. She had substituted many a word association for a fact. After all, her name was a sound she could hide behind. The association was always like a showing.

In her childhood she could smell a library a long way off. There she watched out windows from winter all the way to spring. With little girls in navy coats and stripes on their shoulders—hats with naval streamers—she felt certain familiarity. Soldiers in the radio shepherded them to bed as in the little town of Bethlehem there were blue skies and wolves under the stars. Men, words, woods, books—they were all the same.

Her forefathers were millers who sold off their daughters like reproductions at a poor man's auction. Like so much paper in the moon's shine, the girls were given away to men, and the churn of the mill went on cutting wood. Foam stuck to the falls, but leaves like fish bellied up on the surface of the slow water. For a while the forefather got sadder, but then he'd get happier again, after turning an invisible corner. He could live without the jingle of her fairy laughter after all!

After she was sold, she was often behind a moving window. The way a sealed maidenhead holds the zero in, she loved being hidden, really uncreated in a day. Why be anywhere at all? she wondered. I might as well be here, she concluded, since I have to be somewhere. Stationed behind glass watching deer and foxes watching man and running. *I have to be somewhere!*

Sexual organs pretend there is a connection to the imagination of the body they are on; there is none. It is a sin a few inches in length to believe there is one (that is, to create a connection). Sin is an inevitable space which falls between the self who is born and the source of that self. Like foreskin it increases with time and with actions which result in either suffering or pleasure. (The need for pleasure, by the way, is life-preserving. But why then do feeling good and being good have so much in common?)

As long as she was alone, she was out of pain and complete. Introduce another person, she was less. This is one reason she worried about something as trite as the position of a beam of light. To have it fall on a wall squarely was similar to having an angel in the house. On the other hand she discovered that being "less" was a way of being lighter, more at liberty, and that having company, or taking on the burdens of another person, actually freed her.

So the complex nature of choice finally dawned on her. She could only suppose that finding the balance was the solution—that is, finding a balance that you knew you couldn't keep.

During a seven year span she waited for her husband to come home—that same father whose fathers sold her down the river. And the thing is, she was in a home NEAR home, not AT home, a fact which certainly affected his ability to find her. It was horrible to see her cursing God and the husband and the father, all in one blow, for failing to find her, when she was the very one who chose to be in the wrong place!

Finally she was alone with her suffering, and suffering is the hardest thing on earth to accept. She had to learn that it is still suffering, even after it has been accepted, before she could accept it. That was a trick. It wasn't that she liked to suffer—who does? It wouldn't be suffering if it gave pleasure—but if she accepted it, she would find her random and finite life meaningless. At least this is what she feared.

Then she remembered childhood. When she was six years old she was led down a garden path, through back yards, and up some steps to her first school. She might have been walking down the aisle to meet her first groom. Joy—anticipation—almost to the point of delirium—these were her states. But no sooner had she entered the brick walls than everything went wrong. She couldn't utter a hello, she was gagged so tight by her own delight. She fell and skinned her knee while jump-roping. The teacher made her drink warm milk. Made her! Her father was late coming to get her—he got lost—so by the time he arrived, she had a bad stomach. But the point of the memory was this: until that day the conditions of being in the world, no matter how peculiar or painful, were acceptable to her small person. After that day, her trust wavered. Institutions conspired to make her a defender of her rights.

It was the last year for many years that she would be free of such notions. Until then, she knew the meaning of home. After then, she began her fear of brick. A square building, buffalo brown, was the start of her fear of brick. The associations she made were like showings—that is, appearances by the soul of truth. She often felt she was at the bottom of a set of stone stairs in a garden. At a window, you can be sure she was always waiting for her father to come home.

To accept the pang his absence caused her was equivalent to allowing burning teadrops to settle on your wrist. A kind of demystification of the facts. Pinching herself. To know she was composed of material as biodegradable as a paper bag from a supermarket. She pinched she. The will to do so was only a symptom of her own self-involvement. The thing was stuck. A closed circuit with nothing to let her out unless she could interrupt one of her first attachments, and start a new set of associations. That might do.

Words would have to go. She tried a different language and said Cogito. But it was still her same tongue—that tongue which took the host of heaven weekly into herself—which uttered the odd word. You could say, she was alive without knowing what life was. Or: because she was alive, she didn't know what life was. That was closer. So she now sensed that nature was the clue, being the perfect and eternally given model of obedience and abundance. (Think of raspberries, roses, snowfalls, waterfalls, birds, the wind in the trees and white flowers!)

Like the vision of a sailboat on the horizon, flying an inch off the sea, she glimmered paradox. What was necessary, absolutely, was impossible, too. There were, for instance, four rules that caused much weeping in the world. They went like this:

Continue to have children even though you know they will not live forever.
Continue to work against poverty, even though you know the poor will be on earth always.
Continue to alleviate suffering, even though you know it will never be eliminated entirely.
Continue to love even though you will be separated, in the end, from the object of your love.

These were the assignments sent up from the heaven inside the person. If she could only send them out and abroad, across the world, she would rest, but words were no longer the ones she could stand behind. She wanted to send them down the falls with her father's timber and chips. But such an action was not built into her system.

LAURA MORIARTY

SPICER'S CITY

when like palms with life
lines crossed as if memory
also didn't last

        you along the street seen

        dripping with trees

        the mind bright

We talked so long it burned my back. We never talk. My throat is bare.
The sun. Never there. Day or night.

or white but not
like this stone ball
or like this record
round

The world in your town drenched as they say. Speaking about absence.
There is a register. A blur. A child tearing through the street. Not like
you either.

        high afternoon haze

        your day to be home

        In your day

is language strangely. You ask yourself what it will take. That taken. In the same words. A boy feels along the walls as if he were blind.

they take him

they taste him

angrily

The street is torn apart. The old street hidden and changed and hidden again. The new material. We don't sing. Our steps thrown back. The pavement as white as the sky. Hell with the women these flyboys.

                              but you are no pilot

                              we sit in Gino & Carlo's

                              at midday

The livid tables green as the child I mean what I say "We are not alone here." The music is identical. The pipes moan. There is less water than before. There is no rain at all

like real rain

I have not forgotten

we sound

the same when we say the same things like people of a certain time. As if history were not over. This is about the neighborhood of objects we are in. Someone is here. Is not here. It can be written the same way. It can't be said.

Black fish in paper bins. Water as clear as the sea. A boy playing hide and seek. A small boy. A large ceramic tree. He seems lost without you. He feels nothing.

> yet as time
>
> pretending to be
>
> you or I

Frankly I have come here for you. Some things are brutal. There will continue to be works about gardens but this isn't one of them. This is the real world. Or is this the world? Do I have time for a quick one before whatever passes for night around here passes?

> distant bit of roof
>
> pink and red pales
>
> wall of gold

Chinatown finds itself open. All this silk. The old patterns imagined again burning. Torn or thrown away. Acres of it. Children dancing crazily to bells. No one tells them.

> moon of iron
>
> rock garden steps
>
> am tired boy

oak and palms tried

Like criminals we

know too much. A deserted watering hole in the deserted West. The
Polk Gulch. The Mediterranean sun divides its victims. Each searches
for the other one. And I can still feel the burn. The new set of words.
Obvious in its disguises. I have pictures of the empty room.

unconscious quotation

broken like bones

they were yours

Gay bones. Jay De Feo eyes. On both sides of you naked. Your face. Ca-
pable of anything. The accident of putting two things together. Any
two. Any time. It's territory day in the islands. Also your fault.

gone all out

prediction

A man takes his breath in and I decide to get it back out again.

love of

Oh!   Poor Girl!

The scale is the same. The space between house and ancient building choked with greenery. The moist air between us. The con men play with each other. A hero is trapped in a pinball machine. You are driven away with.

Poor taste

is never enough. My fever shakes this picture of trees. Blooming. Not everything that doesn't exist is me. I have nothing to explain. That seems shallow but goes in. Contains blood. Is round. The steaming tar like lava makes the new town.

the figure with strings

strung

A mannequin in a window manipulates a doll. Caught in the act of being motionless. Her head turned away. Inasmuch as it is a head. He seems to fly. His arms held out. They are arms. Our arms. It follows with the logic of a false similitude left from another age. We believed in that too. Christ what innocents. Whose will go first?

Like firecrackers in the Broadway Tunnel. The continuous roar between things. He claims not to understand negative space. The soft skin. The mute discipline no one is ready for. We say nothing to each other. Day after day. The celebration is ruthless. There is a musical version of the past.

caught in the radio

is constant danger

Also I am

constant also caught. The indecipherable note pasted like a rose to the wall barely lit by the sun going down. I have gone down. Is clear to someone. Or like a castle under siege. Overgrown with Edenic trees. The worse for the wind raging above this solidity. Things made of stone subject only to the catastrophes we know don't change things. Or change completely but we remain unshaken. We are the objects. The people were destroyed. More than once.

> we were just words
>
> like the pear is a fruit
>
> and is yours

and is filled with sun like the valley with the white roses pictured here. You can almost see the heat. The petals blurred as if unsure of themselves. The rain also pictured.

rains

naked from the waist

smokes or steams

Because the heat is relentless. It never rains when it's hot here. Petals for eyes. Something new pasted over the new thing. A child holds you to its lips. A highrise where the hotel. Also of granite.

A burned-out pit. Graffitied man alive at the bottom with what did you expect next to him. They would laugh if they knew. Our grotto written in red paint. A tent made of paper. The moon is still empty. But it will never be like it was. Known not to exist. The new moon.

is midday

We lay down in the lightest possible sun. She sang while it was too hot to move. But now it's not. Kwannon ice white Chinese goddess of love. Old red flowers turning yellow. Things disappear in the fog. He referred to certain people as the neighborhood.

still here

we are gone

This is the series of stone steps that don't go on. The animals squirming.

FROM: **EASY WINNERS**

An arrested story, a narrative of some
meaning, not intended not needed as simply
told, the details of a life. Familiar foods and
universal truths, spoken low when the heart does
love. Here seeks love reaction and touch
becomes a preposition (loves requirement)
into
where
out of the
A twinkle in her eye, a house with no
face legs pointed firmly, arms waving,
eyes like touching pools

The sand becomes colloquial, a swell face
all of our bodies lean toward the tenements
next town. Daddy took out the universe
Cows moo toward home. Why did you see
that sky? A Japanese sunset, the villagers in
Taiwan, the French bourgeoisie curious
how they taunt and dream. Little Buffy
won't lick her milk. He throws his volatile
stars across the court. They scatter and
wrap the sky. The gut is given and yet away.
A tender dove while certainty washes uninterrupted.
We are left as the heart vanishes. The
dunes at midnight, and always the dawn at
the window of the upper class. Always the
bordering dream as if coming thru it suggests freedom

See how they play. The cheese stands alone.
The heart swells methodically like hanging drops
of light.
     Turn now and become.
     Wade and spin.
Not anatomy into action, sweetness of hands
delicate. Women finally got
the word. Do you ask? Is this it?
Do you want to know? Do you need to ask?
Does it need to be more direct? Is it
clear? Are you getting it? Is it in
the same language? Are you sure?
Do you see it? Do you hear it?
Are you answering it? Is it enough?
Are you ready? Are you there? Is this
the right vernacular? A lot of women
poets impaled from the Chinese? The little
wolves on the outside. The hurtling future
voice of these hers. Almost a phenomenon
     Once said – where else what
release. My arms enfold with change. Her
voice in the ancient sense. Our birds they
do lie down and yet a slew of
them take flight.
     Oh the dreamer flying out of the
cave listens to the simple heart. Can you
hear it? The tribe aligns itself in a
perfect stance. A perfect sadist
ready to unfold. As if an army was being
invented. Ready to undo the crumbling
of the push pull – so early on.
Red rope outstanding to swing on
push pull early in the day. Eyes

systematically checking. Sometimes the
body is a resting place. Turn and shout
work and play.
     A monitor, the collective lover
pummeling. We would go and want to know.
How many ways of making it. A lesser
known singer. All week of Baby baby
only baby. Oh baby my sweet baby
Robert John follows his baby down
the nursery babies, Baby love, baby beware
the french babies cool as ice, Here baby
You'll always be my baby, Diane Ward's
baby, the baby at the age of 6 months
the infant, the baby of your dreams,
when you were a baby your mother
and father loved you very much, Do you
think the baby knows it's dreaming. It's popular
now to have a baby. My baby loves to
dance. My baby does it so good. Here comes
the baby. Here is your baby. Here you
are acting just like a baby. What a baby. He
acts just like a baby. Do the guys like
to be babied. Oh baby. Why baby. I'm still
waiting on you baby.
     Symbolic attacks of reckless consis
tency. Mistress becomes mastress.
Small gestures of modern life. Shimmering
and widening at the turn of the year.
An unsentimental mystery – who is the
mother and who is the father? Won't they
say it? What to do.
I saw a photo in a magazine the
other day that reminded me of you. They

sat in an old attic – the door opened
toward them. The other photo presented another
lying on a bed one's head resting on the
other's shoulders. Two pairs of legs stretched
out. The mood was one of contentment
and surprise. There they were soft and
resilient And when I looked at
it part of it was as us. And yet the light
Bold primary stripes of color, fist raised
over the portrait of Mao.

  Scarletta, Katrina, Treemonisha. The names
of the word. Beloved, vigilant, tyrant or waterfall.
The world so large and tender
A big sigh and yet away
Everyone is quiet and near.
Now come away my lovely cat.
Some women in actuality
continued driving notes far from the destination.
A soul of lost boys being followed
climbing the ladder far up into the night.
Some words find that place.

FROM: CONVERSATION PIECES

Magical Thinking

Once upon a time
neither nor speaks
bearing the burden of your words
thumb rubs forefinger
wish it away

Colors

Short guys as bosses
extra harmony
lust for happiness
push pull

Dog Poem

In every poem
the good old
dog –
I hear the wolf is down
cracker jack
immediate vs. daily
life

Day 1

Improvisation
of the new
wasted on history

working the world
every day

The Magic Box

Somewhere in the magic
box
the image of his son looks directly
into his eyes

Mastery

Doubled over
play is their work
opening towards the heavens
birds make their perfect way

Self Protection

Gathering *rounds* of deep feeling
misguided eloquence of the noble war
based on "to die for you"
where your body is in space
thought snapped
Is that what you want?

Where You Live

On the edge of
self protection
under the archway
in thru the door

Archways

Cathedrals of wild beasts
spaces in the house of charity
everything on the inside
lazy swollen tears

Age Appropriate

Where her body stops
and theirs begins
Buster move

Easy Winners

Falling over back into
childhood
little chickens cluck
lively on the living
floor
solace gleans like
an alien moon

House of Dreams

In the house of
dreams
all the rooms are
painted green

ALAN DAVIES

PANTHER

for Elfriede Steck

Frogs croak in the pond
at the end of the road
which rightfully ends at a hillock of stone.
Debussy's *Preludes for Piano*
and crickets in among the frogs.
In the same breath.

———————

Small insect sounds fill up the night.
Moths beat repeatedly against whatever covers light.
I find myself swatting at mosquitoes, just like before.
That dog Mike comes
and protects us from a daydream of bears
because we let him eat.
A couple of shots of cognac
ride nicely as the last Ravel notes out.
There's more to life than either luck or habit.

At night the leaves turn up in the wind to catch the light
thrown by the ending fire.
My mind is as clear as a rainbow
when it sees a rainbow.

I like to watch the clouds foaling in the mountain passes
and how they blanket the green of trees into scenery.
Shoals of light are shouldered off just by the clouds being there
even at this time relatively late in the day.
For a while we're completely encased in the clouds with the birds.

Moths leave at the first bit of wind
and the mosquitoes drop at the first drops of rain.
Soon I have to go back to the city
and find who I can work with, and by working with them win.

A tiny yellow spider insect flies straight at my waiting face
and then hovers off into the near middle distance,
just another thought.

A medium brown moth just avoids the coal stove.
To do nothing is more than enough at anybody's height.
Mosquitoes know the sound of one hand clapping.
Everywhere there is existence in this night
and existence that escapes this night.

There's nothing like the curdling love of our cold friends to dampen
        our weekend.
You know who you are even if you come by here years after we're gone.
We're fully prepared for your dawning absence
and for what glitters and passes for memories under your feet.
It's dew in the porch light. Come back soon.

So many ageless little beetles
are dying tonight
and a moth the size of two eyes' lids
comes begging for the light.

Outside there is nothing but darkness
and the reflection of this inner room in light.
Someone sleeps beside me although she's far from home.
Was it only yesterday a man spoke to me in German beside a lake
that will always float in time without a name?

I marry myself to a mountain tonight,
the one I'm on.
There must be an owl down in the swamp across the road
or perhaps it's a heron. I don't know.

————————

And now there are other sounds in the house
from those after we'd come and I swept the porch
free of leaves that had fallen since we left.
You could at that time hear a lone leaf drop
if you had been here, dearest Steve in the indigo west.
About the forest, what can one say? The sun has to set somewhere.

————————

Poetry can't convey the red of the leaves through the pines
but as night comes it doesn't need to.

————————

How is it that some of our friends are further along the path than we are?
Of course we all bear lumber in our hearts
as a way of being something for the world to look through.
Who knows this more cautiously than the man who lends his heart
        to his friends
when all we ever cared for was sending this same thing forward into
        the trenches of sentient comprehension.

There are no spring willows that don't have dust at their feet
and no poems that don't bear the thin filament of longing at their start.
Until we unstitch ourselves from the long crowds of men
how will we ever know that we'll get back in again?
We're the biggest intruders on this scene.

———————

The sky is clear of clouds tonight except where the moon picks some
out.

The snow is just snow on the ground and the lower sky is not clear of
trees but the trees are entirely clear of leaves.

Tessie is in the hot green bathtub and this is my mind as it studies or
rests.

———————

We see the moon dip out before us
and wonder at the stars.
There's a flight that kind of hungers over the snow
but what are we in this bliss of a momentless moment?
There's no answer but the sketches of answers walk all over the stones.
And then again if I get up to get a cigarette.

Hunky dorey, little love. You and me, out of the same stream and the same flowering.

The night sky got much brighter when the music out of Thelonius stopped.

Elfriede was right. It's a full moon and it's snowing. There's a patch of ground with no snow on it and there doesn't appear to be any reason for that.

We've only been here two hours and I'm already a little bit drunk. What will it be like in twenty years?

———————

All night the sky hungers for a few herons
and the trees crack and stumble in the wind.
Some brute with four feet has knocked the bird-feeders down.

———————

FROM: **THE WHOLE NOTE**

Stop and way eager to follow a yellow bird. A little dry

seeded where the seed fell absolute. The nothing intimate alone in broad day clapped the door behind me, shot out on own free will. Fox is not always easily

my name, to irritate my man. Power over wants to stroll all puffed up, a caricature. My disagreeable bifurcation as well. Tiring to cleave

aback moss, shade and distance. Were to work it off hung of the crowd, timed by seasons of rain. Your injury opportune only as support can wax. Otherwise, I'm still looking for parables

light away. The house and settlement are empty, destined their inhabitants. Sharpen my plan, an image of hunting.

———————

Each sustained gaze deflected, feminine for shame. Contemplative or active operation on a wave from multiple to indicated tread water resists through indirection. Unbalanced to the next

without a subject, belonging elsewhere. What profit from a poem, or picking starfish from the hair

of one collapsed at last stagger. Water is one fills the concave on the corpse removal, is many

sensate at play, fools surviving in a column of words. Clarifying anger adoring gold, at a little fish beached a principle affirmed and broken. Break off sleep to sleep purposeful wander.

Bark and fennel stalk destroyed, scattered scent winding in the same field the violent

macadam, wires and traps. Monotone and irrational acts listen this bag of ribs is letting wind! By hurry

mean debacle at hand. Transform in habits a colony, tests his vocal cords, cries out at the people who invented him. In every case the imperative case

too to wait for rain and be a part of nothing. Muscle in the skin pull to a gait presence, even

surface and interior. Night is more familiar, run ordered there. Lacking breath, redirect wit.

———————

His own neighbor to appear himself uplifted, and elsewhere, victim of the theft erodes way of going under. I meet him on an isolated corner, we exchange

punctuation to intelligible adjustment, through his eyes. Compare paranoia, twice

old bird out of hell to ruminate alone. Up and express my will his habits contemn my knowledge of his failing

exposed. In his ease ended those listening as well, a board stick jammed where bone had been, the crown of a tooth

spat blood, or rum, collapsing, then standing again. The steps, once lost, are never exhausted. The youthful look a drug deserts wants in, that is, out with me, from here.

———————

Full of paper's bobcat spot verified by previous sightings. The cat's intelligenced a man of the state where none was sustained. Danged friable paths and utter

fixed attends a slight sway, a quick glance left and staple on. Bulk obscured by chaparral, that dried by drought, a shuffle the weight

tread and threat preparing. Ennerved pace like the earth a minute

two, there, by the scent, flanks exposed. The text is nothing, not even waiting. Taste lost sleep

a tense identity violating mere whereabouts, careful to back off still. An apt slip, game, and the brush runs by.

Not that it can't be, but I can't tell you. Disturbance to my foot print scrapes narrative assumptions, breath knuckled by labor. Analyse "disturbance" and find its regularity

proven in the inhabitant need. Solidity the aura reminds an absence a place to hide. The molted

annual crop leaps. Fog from skirts tiny warm differential peeps, a kind of secret, vestige

surviving out of the picture. Nourishment and patience fall shadow to your eagerness to know. Length a day out under camouflage, attributed odors daily twists out of reach. Sink a lair, decay.

I make a sound. I am out of breath, always, my sound becoming a complaint, my complaint

hump, moving through the fog. Fear asleep swim obsessed with enforcing rhythm. Wounded and taken, held

to own a scar, pilloried to be fed is no possession. I to those I associate adventure and routine, uncertain in memory. From them one, all of us available

at distances uncommonly dissolved. Black in my eye, gone, an angular trespass frozen against me. Night's water's cape, have at me, all you want, exhaust and further.

Another man, a woman, with effort, confess effort physically construed. The breathing

column parallel truths lain by the expiring do, what must be done. Walking in silence, at ability joyous, to muscled speech. Operative we, the varieties of pace argue and agree

height, endurance, knowledge of causes sure to divide we bring and bring it up without departing. What difficulty

spurious flight, glide beckoned, the crevice, creek and marsh coincide. Certain light disturbance or character of wind to human presence, full of face constituted, abbreviated choice. We to they web carrion, walking still.

MEI-MEI BERSSENBRUGGE
AND RICHARD TUTTLE

HIDDENNESS

Remarks derived from a showing of our collaboration, *Hiddenness,* at Intersection in San Francisco, May, 1990. Mei-mei Berssenbrugge alternates with Richard Tuttle.

1.

I like to write for collaboration, because it gives a different density to the writing. You can use the other person as an energy source, without exploitation. I enjoy trying to be able to discern what a whole would be, and then to fill in.

In collaboration, *the theme is love, and, paradoxically, you try to make a work of art with another person.*

2.

I use the whole other person and the whole situation as well as the particulars of a project. I wrote *Hiddenness* for images Richard showed me, and also to what I thought was behind these images in him.

Before I began *Hiddenness, I tried to make a book by myself. A red line circled each page of this book. This red line, though invisible in* Hiddenness, *is the hidden source that makes the collaboration possible.*

3.

Trying to write to the images, you have to feel your way past literalness, to a place in writing where energy gives back and forth between the visual image and text. Sometimes the text goes ahead or behind the images, as in conversation. You don't repeat or translate the other person.

Collaboration is interesting *at the beginning of this decade, because of the plane of consciousness. I feel we are driven to get everything onto one plane* *of consciousness before we go into the next century. Any page of our collaboration could have been a painting stuck to a wall, but if you hold it against a wall, it dies. If you want to see it alive, just take it a few inches away from the wall. It becomes plane of consciousness.*

4.

In placing these long-lined stanzas on a narrow page, Richard also needed to find a space that would give energy back. In this case he calls the new space, "a new idea of literature," breaking the "dead-end" integrity of the page. I think he made a landscape space out of the page, connecting the literary and visual. This space of the page we found is my favorite part of the collaboration.

When you do a collaboration, *it's impossible to achieve the maximum you want by starting from scratch. It's more a form-in-action to be sustained by practice. In fact, it's best if the individual project is totally forgotten, only practice remembered.*

5.

One question we asked, what would show if you poured huge "impractical" amounts of energy into making a book? The edition, 120, is at the edge of what can be handmade and what requires technology. The people who did the printing, the handstamping, the papermaking, the silkscreening, fueled by our vision of the project, contributed great amounts of effort over several years. Now, for me, if you open this book, light pours out of it. It is a kind of paradigm of the value of this kind of project.

The polarity between artists and writers *early in this century, in which artists were anti-nature and progressive, until now, when writers are these things, makes livres d'artistes wholistic. The book for me is conservative, and for Mei-mei progressive. But where one may have been interested in making a whole, now it may be more interesting how these polarities join as an idea for the future of "whole."*

6.

Inspired effort, rather than didactic effort, struggled to pull "book-making" from a sub-culture up to real culture.

When one reads a text *in collaboration with a visual that works, a kind of magic takes place where a little piece of molecule at the edge of any letter can transfer to a little piece of the visual, and energy flows. If that is the result of a labor of love, it is also like a drug, once taken, forever required of love: one knows what's in the house.*

7.

Decisions were made towards aliveness. For example, the indigo of the end pages is organically derived. It then includes your own body, because the skin of the hand against the page is beautiful, which is dead next to chemically-derived indigo, and so excluded from its space.

The problem of an illuminated text is set, *where the problems of an illustrated text are free to move. It's not quite correct to say, "Richard Tuttle: Illuminations," unless the subject were becoming greater than the text itself, but it opened up the possibility that the text was illustration for the text, and this would leave my work, "illuminations."*

8.

"Everyone knows you can't look while you're thinking." We addressed an antipathy between the visual and literary. I can't think while I'm looking. Richard thinks this century is trying to unify the visual and literary planes of consciousness. Making this new space on the page is trying to do this.

When one member is in *the magical space that is the collaboration, they will never know what the other one is doing. It's strange, this space, for it is crystal clear, yet hides the invisible. Later a collaborator may know how hard the other worked, and will say, "I didn't know it at the time; I suppose that's that kind of magical space."*

9.

There are several physical planes of meaning in the book, that unify a meaning out of its construction. There are the areas of colored pulp in the paper itself, then, the incision of typesetting below or into the paper, then the hand stamping that is applied onto the paper.

Marcel Broodthaers found a connection *between the literary and the visual. In an exhibition called "The Eagle" in 1970, he installed objects he had collected of or about eagles. To each object, he added, "This is not a work of art," in French, English, or German. The connection between the visual and the literary is both a relationship and a set mode. The mode has a character that can move with time. You can plug into it anew, like placing a light farther down track lighting. Today, this relationship is in a different place than for Broodthaers.*

10.

You're trying to make something with another person, which would be a metaphor for a relationship, using an essential quality of a social species, so you have a deep resonance underlying collaboration. Plus the tension of the insularity of works of art in our time.

They say an artwork is always *revealing new truths. And also, the best books can be read over and over. How are these the same? How are we capable of combining the two in collaboration? How are we closer to what each is saying in collaboration, than alone? How are we capable of finding the end of art in between them, as form?*

Hiddenness, published by the Whitney Museum Library Fellows in 1987, can be seen at the Whitney Museum Library, The New York Public Library Rare Books Collection, and The Getty Center for Research of Art and the Humanities.

HIDDENNESS

1

Though relations with oneself and with other people seem negotiated in terms secretly confirmed

by representations, her idea of the person's visibility was not susceptible to representation. No matter

how emphatically a person will control his demeanor, there will be perspectives she cannot foresee or
   direct.

because there is no assignable end to the depth of us to which representation can reach,

the way part of a circle can be just the memory of a depth. The surface inside its contour,

like the inside of a body, emits more feeling than its surroundings, as if

the volume or capacity of relations would only refer to something inside, that I can't see,

that the other person and I keep getting in the way of, or things in the landscape while they are
   driving,

instead of the capacity being *of* your person.

2

If the tree is crimson in the fall in the mercury light by the river, I feel it gather its color *from* the river.

An orange moon is partially hidden in the clouds in the darkness.

Whenever or wherever it is possible to speak of recognition, there was a prior hiddenness or border *of* the circle,

where private means you would not be able to understand, as if understanding the possibility *of*

were veering slashes of light on a steep track. It is more like driving without headlights on the plain,

the moon's appearance of a lake by a power plant, a dead lake, whose color neither hides nor doesn't hide

a perspective. I would call it color, if the way the texture of the skin on his hand

changes in moonlight were a color, instead of fantasy,

so that the physical idea of his privacy is not made clearer by the idea of his secrecy.

It is the same sentence as trying to explain how her assessment could not wait for her uncertainty.

You could be hiding behind a pane of glass in the atmosphere, or an example inaccessible to what

you are hiding, the way the beauty of a person, during a daydream, may flash across your mind, like an animal across the landscape, forcing an exclamation from you, when you might not remember its name.

3

She is not the name of a person, nor there of a place, but they are connected with names.

There is a way of traveling by rotating an orientation, while she remains within herself.

He moves his hand across the shadow and it tints delicate skin on the back of his hand. He has a doll in his mind on which he can predict what she will be feeling, as if he would not touch the doll, until her actual feeling would make contact with the object of his thought.

Why science does not use a word like she or there, is why the hand cannot make a sharp edge in the sand.

The hollow his hand would make in bright sun, micaed, was the place where the wing of the person would fold into itself, almost a shadow in skin. The fold is an object or resemblance between the head turning over a shoulder, and the wing folding.

He touches her shoulder at the place where the wing would begin, while she is sleeping.

She can concentrate on the objects in the room, and his talking to her, but the context is of losing
    herself

in possibilities like vowels, or birds during a period of plastic song, in which syllables are repeated
or rehearsed over and over. The head turns and lays itself in a hollow of skin along the ribs,

like a color onto the back of his hand, which could be one of her own thoughts.

It's how a seed would germinate and be free of its blood, as in a hive or a galaxy,

pervading the atmosphere, like ambiguity before a conception.

You have the sense of a color of a cheek. Your sense of the colors of the heart moving

is the assessment of a turning point, that curves over territory like an edge of light,

or the oxygenation of an emotion, bypassing the doll.

4

If one string line of a bone crosses another properly, an area of brightness or intensity is created, so
that a skeleton, because it was hidden, appears to have been exposed, almost inadvertently

in the stance of a young boy who had been extracting a splinter from his foot that was resting on his knee, his hands

grasping the delicate foot. He makes a seamless extension from the space of the canyon into her mind.

Does seeking a cause make a line tremble, an act of the eye and the light, so that a space

will not stretch so immovably, nor each rock place itself as individual?

Can "a cause" occur on the skin of his fingertips, instead of along fissures of your thinking,

reflecting the brightness of a line, without the idea of the line?

She suspects his relations with his own mind may spark intuitions, which force him to pass over any attempt to say anything to himself. Not as a child would throw a ball out of its crib, and you would carry it back. He would like to pass something over to one side that does not come back, such as the more complicated a question, the less light would come back, until no light comes back. You would know everything you see in the first place, but the terms of your recognition grow increasingly intimate and ecological, like the light of the gold of jewelry on you, which, while it is still light, is still becoming abstract.

A creature walks on the quiet floor of the canyon, a dry floor, sparking with mica, under which water flows,

and turns its head aside from a thorny bush with red seeds hanging down. The light is so bright its volume would be a source to see whiteness from, which falls on a hand or on jewelry differently.

If she walked to the edge of the canyon and looked down, the creature would pass twelve feet below.

Like an image, it would absorb her interest, or like an oxygenation along the miles of the insides of its living cells. The creature is a motive which could generate an image of her own body disappearing and appearing again after an interval or length of the canyon.

This occurs center stage with footlights illuminating it, where she is the footlight.

She can trace paths through the space of a canyon, generating a motive of it which to light a case where there would be some way of applying the color, like some form of light projection, saturating or fusing all the particles at all levels of the insides of their capacities.

It is how the ghost of an image was made to appear in his mind. What he can feel about a red, and how far and how deeply are not matters of what feeling "a reason" causes in her.

The human being, troubled by limits, creates a trip for herself, a honeymoon, which recreates her

as spacious. Now, she projects expanse onto endeavors, such as the representation of an angel,

or the way the colors of the world would lie over the world, a pleasurable collation of objects

as of hues of the shadow of an emergence place.

It passes a richness of seeing or believing back onto the impasto of the colored things,

in which anyone else may mean anyone other than the two of us, or anyone other than you, and you
will go,

who are the color of a seam, and not a doll

of painted biscue which makes matte protuberances or patches of invisible places across a space.

A cloud in the morning folds over a monument on the plain, a vector like an avalanche of mist
concealing it.

She creates a dark flank of a mountain, a person's thoughts or feelings passing across the person,
concealing the person.

She wonders what the body would reveal, if the cloud were transparent.

It pervades the creation of a motive, like the action of a heart.

COUNTERMEDITATIONS

1

Slow down
and the insects catch up with you.
Slow down even more
and they fly right past you
mistaking you for a wooden stump.

2

An insect writing
would appear immobile
to a human.

An insect writing
to a human
would appear immobile.

A human writing
would appear immobile
to an insect.

A human writing
to a human
would not appear.

3

Two people kiss,
go off together.

What happens next
is on them.

4

When a city looks at a person
it sees only the sky.
Rivers flow through the city,
light consumes them.

5

One size fits all—
the ring
the wheel
the stash . . .

Hanging out
on the periphery
of occupation

I sounded it out
to hammer sounds
in leaf shade

moving with the wind.
A man was working
on an addition.

Vapor trail
like a giant eyebrow
over clouds, houses,
trees, ditch, fence,
and picnic table top—
fans out
into light blue.

6

Between a rock
and a soft spot
unity
and virtual fragmentation

the United States Postal Service
Commemorative Stamp Club
makes its presence felt
on the eclectic American plain.

7

If all words
were blown away,
which words
would be the first
to recur?

Does what's said
grow like a sprout
from silent earth?
Or is it a belt

in a moving assembly
of words?

"yes"
"hot"
"way"

Slowly at first
building a house to last
corners cur
in the ongoing course of events

the way I figure
and the way interruptions collide
the body turns over
sleep startles the owner
in time to wake with all things.

8

You have completely mastered everything.

Now what ! ?

9

Our life is composed
of fragments
stitched in sleep.

Days weave the light
skin tight against the thought
of which our life is composed.

10

I got one of your moons today.
The space behind it whitened and went out.

These words occurred to me
somewhere in Helsinki.
They seemed to come from you.

I showed them to you
and you said you might take them back,
to which I agreed, absentmindedly.

FROM: 3: SHAPE

We tell each other stories to alter the image of things. Some schisms are meant to be empty. Why else would we peer through a magnifying glass and use monosyllables. Now we start over . . .

––––––––––––––

At the bottom of a cup of coffee two photographs. One of a woman in a diner, in the background people screaming. The other is blurred, but the image of a man on a Ferris Wheel is distinguishable. He is not screaming but the people around him are. The telephone rings, the cook answers it and begins shouting. Three stools down a man stares absently at the order tags whirling around on the silver wheel the cook puts in motion. Two people on the street collide and raise their hats in anger. Tomorrow I meet his camera.

––––––––––––––

A person in the dark placed between two rows of floodlights. Clips of us in strange costumes performing unnatural acts. Others arrive impersonating machines, taking part before it is broken up and we are sent away to our respective opposites.

––––––––––––––

I change my name every spring. I might use fionnula in the future, or Sam. You used Sam several years ago. Not that I'm trying to be emulative—Sam's clothes suit me, as does his head. Last time I noticed you were using Taylor, because of Robert, and grew taller. Taylor carries a pocket watch and flips it open, checking the reflection in the crystal, to make sure.

———————

You wanted to inhabit that thing believed to be "me." I offered you perfect white teeth and let you examine them. You held them to the light making sure this was it. You decided this was scary and must be a hoax. The alarm went off then, a good time to change the subject. You said, after a pause, that my shoes looked eerie in the open closet, pointed and . . . why are all of them black anyway? Crossing the room, I looked out to the park and you followed me to the window. We watched an ice skater practicing routines on a small pond stumble, then regain her balance. She sat down on a bench, catching her breath, then began again. Her movements now were self-possessed, assured. I smiled what you wanted to see.

———————

It's hard to see back to the beginning of the film. You desire his head on a platter, settle for his watching you dance. Imaginary footlights. Four legs moving to the music. You enjoy the focused attention and how the camera grows larger as you turn gracefully in circles and the film expands into what occurred before, then breaks.

We love the rain; it always seems to be raining. We will be enemies until this is over. Your words, false, burn an idea, the body a protective covering. Emotions dry up over the years. Then sparks appear. Behind someone's eyes desire and resistance are forgotten. Violins like sadness. Or maybe not that way at all. We forget the impetus and add another chair to the table.

Tomorrow, the man in the black hat with swollen genitals. Yellow fleur-de-lis paper on the walls. High ceilings, open transom. The building is old and hallway dark, more so because it is raining. The doorknob comes off in my hand, to be used as a prop.

KAREN KELLEY

THE INTERPRETATION OF DREAMS
(VIRTUAL REALITY NO.I)

You go into the garden of artifacts, shells and bones, WHERE YOUR
MAIDENHOOD IS, and find the fault in the crust of it, ten miles you
walk, swearing to get yourself for this betrayal. Cut to an evening land-
scape. SUDDENLY THERE IS NO SOUNDTRACK JUST BEHIND YOU,
SHOOING, SHOOING. Your maidenhood is a curtain from ceiling to
floor—a rough, nubby, indefinite form; first a fleshy, red, edible hat like
a DISTURBING PERSPECTIVE, then a blouse of small towns and suburbs,
a heartland bent in the direction the wind blows, its side view suspend-
ed from your neck and used as a divining rod in such a way that one
side is lower than the other. Interval of TREMULOUS SOUNDS OF BIRDS,
then a confused teenage girl in a blonde wig suspended above the stage,
foretelling future events by handling distorted perceptions by moon-
light. Thunderheads motionless as flat-bottomed boats bloom over the
lowlands, gradually coming into full view as ALPHABETIC AND NUMER-
IC SYMBOLS, PUNCTUATION MARKS AND MATHEMATICAL SYMBOLS
WITH GOLD VEINS. Books with blurred titles rain down on a bird-bel-
lied, open-mouthed man who takes two pails lined with reflective eyes
and begins to fetch water, and does not step once only, but many times
into the river that comes right up to your body AND INTO YOUR
MOUTH. CLACK OF HIDDEN BUGS. Their beauty lies in actually consist-
ing of brightly colored folds of skin intertwined with twigs for legs. The
Birdman loosens and LETS FALL IN DISARRAY ACROSS THE TABLE your
hair, your lies, and the towel you use for drying dishes. When you touch
down, you see a man cleansing and dressing stunted forms above tree
line as the lightning combs the sky—that is to say he is using a wooden
peg THAT EXPANDS AS A RESULT OF INTERNAL PRESSURE, which, if
eaten, gives man immortality (that is to say he is using a pear-shaped

muscle that fills with emotion, which, if eaten, causes loss of inno-
cence). THIS IS THE PLOT IN ITS ENTIRETY. Screeches and loud, inartic-
ulate sounds. A wild, uncultivated garden. THOUSANDS OF BABIES,
blinking, dressed in brainwaves and nerves, lacy bonnets pulled down
tightly over dyed-red hair. BABIES LIKE BIOGRAPHIES IN THEIR LITTLE
BOXES OF SLEEP, hands collapsed and twilight all around. Glowing like
mystical worlds, their dead centers are thick-lipped mouths enlarged
like photographic images and ADAPTED FOR FEEDING FROM YOU. A
young man (someone you know, a stranger) stands for ten men. The
waiter of German origin. The gardener with his apple-green bones. ETC.
A screen door slams open so you can be the picture, the very *idea* of two
people alone, BACKS TOWARD THE AUDIENCE, aching with a series of
question marks. Even now, he is jerking out pale arms from his wings.
Other men wearing waxy, water-repellent cutaways interrupt the conti-
nuity of the main action by throwing shots of SCANTILY DRESSED
WOMEN into the road where they give the impression of depth and
thickness, of life, fragrance, and magical power . . . then someone starts
to hula. IT IS YOUR FATHER (someone you know, a stranger) dressed as a
strong, muscular, virile man. He has a rich, chewy beard. Gauzy, black-
spotted cherry-blossoms SPURT FROM THE TREES. Capricious flames
like animals consume persistent, illogical feelings which are not pretty
to the eye: the flames look like a fine net of gestures or a woman's loose
unbelted dress. Creosote bush, bleeding heart and hawthorn, sansevieria
(Oh, costly blossoms produced by sublimation, YOU PAY THROUGH
THE NOSE FOR THEM!) Up close, they look like sunken leather vessels
full of double meanings that swell when wet. And of course from such
confusion THERE IS NO RETREAT.

GEOFFREY O'BRIEN

FROM: **THE ARMY**

ownership
of the sun
testifies

the uprooted mountain
leafs
into names

the river the ankle
the hatch
the shrub the talon

prison calendar
work squad
trench rope

a thatch gap
harbor depth
rock view

water storage
vocabulary
for conquest

wrests from eyes
the border line
palpates

flayed eagle
corrosive
sexual flower

an emptying
by night's end
of habitable stone

swept out
of fluid city
a blood anthem

raucous
died in sight of
a rooster

language dissects
a marsh
binds the frost

an invaded air
chapel
primary salt

blesses the birds
the foxes tills
fences off

angelic
shell scrapings
azure waste

split harbor
dissolved
the letters

a line of beaks
flint stubble
friendless

crow starved

watchman they died

at night

in brook sting

washed

weathered

no time for memory

to hoist

the empty flank

tracking a variance

in the horizon

the mutilated

underbrush secured

teach savages

to worship

shred books

the flax

and stoneware mute

obedient

gangs a manuscript

sealed bladed

specifies locks

and pits the unmooring

guarded

they erected interiors

the lookouts

half-napping shrug

orders

to watch

the fireflies

thick back of

the crushed stones

the sky soggy

feverish nothing

wakes the penis

of the archbishop

their wine joke
bastard king
the poor burned

souls a giggle
not me the hawk wing
capacious

mother's song
a charm a village
its names

eaten up the air
rots the sentries
encumber

fever armies
in drydock
maggory

east of harbor
talk noise
before bleeding

wash of bodies

picked over

in noon swarm

inseparable

swamps

brilliant vines

salvaging song

the willow bridge

moor maid

hoarse in fumes

the air packed solid

an Asia

of warning boughs

FROM: A LECTURE AT THE NAROPA INSTITUTE, 1989

What I'm going to do is go through this motley assembly of my published books and explain to you what the structures of the books are. I'm not going to talk about any other aspect of the book except the structure, the form of the work, which I'd prefer to call structure since that's more architectural.

This is the first book I ever published. I published it myself. It's called *Story.* It has no page numbers. It's about thirty pages. The way it came into being was I wrote a story that was about falling down, tripping and falling down. It was nicely written, experimentally so, but it seemed dull. So I tried to figure out what to do with it; and being a twenty-year-old person at the time, I went overboard and made a structure that is like a diamond shape where I accumulated other texts. I was very interested in American Indian myths at that time so I included a Kwakiutl myth about hats and about smoking; their description of a hoop and arrow game; and then an Italian folk tale about fourteen men who went to hell; another Italian tale about a man who sold cloth to a statue; then from Coos myth texts, a story of the five world makers, and the man who became an owl. Then I accumulated some lists from the dictionary of other words for beginning, middle, and end. There's a recipe for true sponge cake, there's a 19th Century letter about etiquette, a couple of quotes from Edgar Allan Poe, and an article by the biologist Louis Agassiz about coral reefs. Each of these things I thought was relevant to the diamond shaped nature or accumulation of the story. Smoking, and cooking. That's all I have in my notes.

As I was saying to Clark Coolidge, there is some aspect of this work that I can't remember (as to how I did it). I took the longest work which was the story I'd written about falling, and I made that begin at the beginning and end at the end. Everything was going on in the exact middle of the work, and at the beginning and end only one thing was going on and it was gradually accumulating and decreasing.

To make things worse, I decided to interrupt the text at random moments with all the words I could think of that would mean story. Here's the list of those. There are fifty-one. (From her reading of the list: anecdote, profile, life-story, scenario, love-story, lie, report, western, article, bedside reading, novel, thumbnail sketch, tale, description, real-life story, piece, light reading, confessions, dime novel, narrative poem, myth, thriller.)

It was interrupted at random. The confluences were amazing. All of a sudden it would say detective story, and the section that was randomly chosen to be a detective story really became one. Or could become one in the reader's mind. Probably more so than in my mind.

(She reads examples of the beginning, middle, and ending definitions). They were interspersed in this text at the beginning, middle, and end.

The structure of the next book is simply the duplication of a journal that I was keeping when I was about seventeen, and it includes translations from Ovid, *The Golden Age,* sort of funny journalistic notes, poems, and things about my grandfather. All I did was print the journal itself, and the reason I did it (I didn't actually do it myself, but the reason I wanted to do it) was because the keeping of this journal was what had inspired me to really want to become a poet. So I thought it would be useful to other people. It's called *Ceremony Latin 1964,* which is the year it was written.

Next comes *Moving,* a book that relates to some people here. Anne Waldman (did you publish it by yourself?) published this book. She discovered me. I went to the country; I had received some inheritance, and I rented a house in Gt. Barrington Massachusetts, someone's summer house that they wanted to rent for the winter. At that point, it was very cheap to do that. I set myself the task of not writing as much as possible. Only writing when I absolutely felt compelled. Never writing in the way most of us do: well I have to write; or I haven't written enough; or I should write everyday. Not doing anything like that, but only that which seems to come from something other than the self. I tried very hard not to write. After a year, I produced this book which Anne discovered as a pile of pages on the top of my typewriter when she came to visit me. She decided to publish it.

The structure of *Moving* is hard to describe except in terms of *this* book. (She holds up *The How & Why Wonder Book of Our Earth.*) I always felt it was important if there are things you don't know about to read good children's books about them and get good explanations as to why the sky is blue. So you really know, instead of reading some abstruse text. So you could really tell somebody. *Moving* is based on the structure of this *How & Why Book,* the table of contents of which reads: The Beginning of the Earth; Upheavals in the Earth; Souvenirs of the Past (that included things about fossils and glaciers); Water, Water Everywhere; The Earth's Surface; Treasures In the Ground; The Underground Rooms (that's all about caves); and The Beginning of Man. That's how I ended *Moving,* with the beginning of man and all of man's talents or lack of them. That's exactly the structure, although the book looks funny. The other thing I should tell you about the structure is that Anne had this nice printer in Williamstown, and he was really very patient. (Anne Waldman says: "Saint.") I told him I didn't want a left hand margin in the book. I wanted it to be raggedy on the left side as well as on the right side. Since he was setting real type, it was almost impossible for him to do that. He said to me, "How do I do it, where do I start the line?" I said "At random," obviously not the right thing to say to a very careful craftsperson. But he did a beautiful job of it. So that's that structure.

Let's see what comes next. *Memory.* Well, this is a complex one too. Notes about *Moving* are in *Memory.* I forgot to tell you, in *Moving* I also incorporated, I solicited work from other poets and writers to include. I invited a lot of people to contribute to the book, whatever they wanted to and I would just intersperse it at random. *Moving* begins with a chance poem to begin from words from ten different kinds of books left in random order but repeatable. That's how the book begins, with this poem that was written in that manner. I used ten different kinds of books, chose random words, and left them in random order but gave myself the right to repeat them. Then I have this note on the back: "I put it all in together. I thought the poem should be information and also political, but not by me. That was an important part of this book, an important political part of the book that it not be written necessarily by me."

This is a book called *Memory*. It originally was a series of photographs. It's a diary of one month. I shot a roll of film, thirty-six pictures everyday. I had a patron at the time, Holly Solomon. She paid for the film and the developing. I shot slides and she made them into prints. She put it up as a show. We did it along the wall; it was about forty feet long and four feet high from left to right as a book would read. I kept journals. We always painted our journals, at the time. I didn't have an automatic light meter, so I kept my list of exposures for the film in the backs of the journals. I wrote incessant notes and made drawings about everything that happened everyday. I wrote down as much as I could without interrupting my life. It was the month of July, 1971. I had chosen the month at random without knowing what I would be doing during that month, because I didn't want to choose a time to do this experiment that would be particularly loaded, or particularly interesting or dull. At the show, all the journals were turned into reel to reel tapes. It opened up in this funny gallery, which was trying to do kind of new things at that point in time. Conceptual art I suppose, is what it's called. So we played the tapes; it was an eight hour show. If you wanted to hear the whole show, you could follow the whole month by walking along with the pictures, and spend eight hours in the gallery.

Praeger Publishers said that they wanted to publish it as a book with all the photographs in it. I thought this was amazing, what a great thing. This agent said, "Can I come and discuss this with you?" and I said, "Fine." He said if you'll make love with me, I'll get the book published.

That's how it wound up in *this* form. So I only have a few photographs in the published book by North Atlantic Books.

Structurally speaking again, when I put the text together I took my journals and I projected the slides on the wall, very small, right next to my desk. When you project the slides very small the colors are very vivid. I wrote sort of around the pictures, around the text I already had, added to it from the pictures. This nearly drove me crazy. One of the reasons I did it was to be nasty to Gertrude Stein who always said you can't write remembering, so I wanted to say to her that maybe you could. I think she's right that you practically wind up in an insane asylum on a project like this. (She answers inaudible question:) Stein has a lot of theories that while you're writing, you should be writing in the present moment or in the continuous present and not be saying things to yourself like "What was I going to say next? Was the couch green or did I say it was green on the previous page?" That sort of thing. It's also a philosophical stance of hers, from her studies with William James. But in a spirit of fun, I was doing it *with* Gertrude Stein.

The next one is *Studying Hunger*. This book is actually two lectures culled from a series of journals. I don't know what to say they're about. What are they about? Hunger? My work with a psychoanalyst. Most of the books are the size of big drawing books. A lot of pictures in them, a lot of colored pens. I knew this was not a publishable work. It's almost masochistic in and of itself to do something like that. When I was invited to give two readings during the years I was keeping these books (there are about seven of them) I took things from the journals and made them into sort of lecture style or lecture length. That's what's in this book. It is a combination of prose and poetry, by Big Sky.

I recently attempted to publish the *Studying Hunger* journals. The publisher balked because there's five hundred pages of text. I'm trying to think if there's anything else I should say about the structure of this book. The combination of poetry and prose and moving freely between both is something that's always been inspiring to me, and especially from reading Dante's *Vita Nuova*. Also, obviously, William Carlos

Williams' *Paterson*. Can anyone think of other books that do that, that move between prose and poetry. Basho. (Students say: *"Desolation Angels."*) Sure. Those are my favorite kinds of books. I love that form. That to me seems like the ultimate freedom. And especially if you have the nerve to analyze your poems after you've put them in the text, as Dante did. He'd say, "And then I wrote this poem" and he gives you the sonnet. He'd analyze them in kind of a dumb way; he tells you what it means, the structure. (Anne Waldman: "What the occasion for it was.") I think it's a great exercise.

The next book, in chronological order, is a book called *Poetry*. I think it's my most boring book. It's divided exactly in half. It was the first time anyone wanted to publish a book of real poems of mine. So I was very excited about the prospect, and I tried to include everything. What I put in the beginning was all my old poems, and in the second section I put the poems I'd written in the last two weeks. That's another possible structure, but I resent the book in a way. (Kulchur Foundation).

Here's a fascinating idea. This book is called *Eruditio Ex Memoria*, which basically means learning out of memory, or learning that is memory. I had thousands of high school and college notebooks that were sitting in a room in my ancestral home. I had to move everything out of that house. Everybody had died. I didn't have any place to put all the things I wanted to keep or save. I thought, regarding the notebooks, they're really all the same in a way. I decided to tear out random pages from each one so I had something from each. I threw the rest away. I took those pages and wrote this book, which is a book really about what you learn in school or how you learn it. The other structural question about this book was how to deal with commas. Because there was so much related material. How to pause, or how not to pause. Here the question was how to make a transition or how to choose not to have a transition.

It's getting easier. As it gets closer to the present, it gets easier. This is really the only real book of poetry I've published. It's called *The Golden Book of Words*. The only structural thing to mention about it is that I chose to keep it in chronological order, because I couldn't stand not having any structure at all. I'm not advising people to do that, just that it often works very nicely to do it.

Next is this book called *Mid-Winter Day*, Turtle Island Foundation, which is one long poem which also includes prose that was written about one day, December 22, 1978. Nobody ever believes me when I tell them that it was written in one day, but it almost was. I did rehearsals for the first section, which is dreams. I practiced for about two weeks before the December 22 date and tried to sort of fine-tune my dreaming so that when I had dreams on the 22nd I would be good at remembering them and they would be vivid and worth recording. Or worth sharing with people; or I would get better at writing them down. So that was an extension over that day. I also took photographs, and wrote about them later.

I divided the book into six parts. It was the six parts of the day, as I perceived the day to be. The last part was the time at night when I would go to my desk and write. For the sixth part of the book, that's what I did. The rest is regular daily doings. I was mostly taking care of babies, and entertaining friends. I also made sure to keep copies of the newspapers for that day and whatever other written or visual material happened to pop up by accident. I'd keep track of it so that when I was putting the poem together later, I might want to intersperse some of that material. But the only real notes I have are those about the photos. Actually I have extensive notes about dreaming but it would be pointless to begin on that.

I wrote this list about the photos (it was one roll of film). I tried to describe what it was before I attempted to use it in the text. "1. Trying to see myself in the mirror over the typewriter as sea. 2. Breakfast at the bottle of milk, white light. Lewis in shirt jacket. Marie stripes putting oatmeal in mouth." I should say that in this instance and also the use of the photographs in *Memory* that I was never trying to take beautiful photographs necessarily. I was always trying to take as many as possible; to take photographs as what you're really seeing, not trying to isolate objects and put them in the center of the frame. But just take them to reflect what actual vision is, and not romanticize it. Certainly not the writing either, but not romanticize the visual.

(She reads other examples.) That's more than you could note in a moment if you were sitting with a notebook. The other thing is that you don't always see all these things when you're looking with your eyes.

It became more information. As I said in the workshop this morning, it would be interesting to write about what you know and leave out the self. I mean for an extended period of time, like a year or so.

Then I wrote *Utopia,* which is red and black. This is another book where I thought it was very important to include contributions by other writers, so there are footnotes and whole sections by other people. Surprisingly, a small number of people actually respond to those requests to be a part of a collaborative writing project. I've worked in workshops and magazines that are collaborative, and it's amazing to see how frightened people are of sharing their anonymity. Being anonymous and sharing knowledge with others.

I wanted to make *Utopia* tongue-in-cheek like a text book with a table of contents, a preface, and index. (She reads from the frontmatter, the essential idea of which is: any part of this book may be reproduced by anyone.) My love of indexes came from a time when I was apprenticing myself to poetry and I decided to write in every form that really couldn't be written. One of those things obviously is to write an index for a non-existent book. (She reads examples from *Utopia.*) Bob Holman created the index for *Utopia.*

Utopia is a form.

This is *Sonnets,* which is my most recent book. It is a book of about seventy sonnets. I was reading a transcript of a Ted Berrigan workshop on sonnets. He apologizes as I do for writing them. After all this work described as experimental and thousands of other manuscripts not even mentioned here, we wind up writing sonnets? Is that what becomes of us? None of the sonnets are really sonnets. A bunch of them that are in the book were originally published in this form called "Incident Reports

Sonnets." A friend of mine works as a psychotherapist at The International Center for the Disabled. Even though it's a place that does wonderful things for human beings, it's very bureaucratic. They pass around memos between offices, such as reporting if a plant has been knocked on its side. My friend would (very much against the rules) give me the incident reports so that I could write poems based on them because they had all the nature of poetry in them. Surrealistically described surrealistic events and everyday things.

Story, 1968
Moving, 1971
Memory, 1975
Ceremony Latin, 1964, 1975
Studying Hunger, 1976
Poetry, 1976
Eruditio Ex Memoria, 1977
The Golden Book of Words, 1978
Mid-Winter Day, 1982
Utopia, 1983
Mutual Aid, 1985
Sonnets, 1989
The Formal Field of Kissing, 1990

BERNADETTE MAYER

FROM: THE DESIRES OF MOTHERS
TO PLEASE OTHERS IN LETTERS,
an unpublished book of a series of letters written but never sent
to people living and dead (nine months, 1979–80).

PLURAL DREAM OF SOCIAL LIFE

Throw stuff away, I've got an apartment above you in the city like food,
I think it's #12A too, a small fast clock. Bigger than I thought with alot
of corners and you bought an extra table for me you left downstairs in
the restaurant, you live just down the street in zoology but when I went
upstairs I saw there was already a nice one in the fast clock and it was
even marble. I wondered if I was going to be able to keep it. Pointless
and from all the windows you can see trees and out one that's broken it's
balloons and a zoo like pointing to a town in northern Colorado or gos-
sip about that, even a misplaced vehemence like you saw on the face of
that guy who came in when you did. Archaic, it wasn't the balloons that
were broken or otherwise how could I have seen them, it sure seemed
like a good place to live because even though you could have described
it accurately as small there was something about it, I could only say it
was full of surprises, and some of them were rooms you could fit beds in
though if you were rich or something you might call them closets, any-
way alot of us could sleep there. Impassivity, I was surprised and things
were better for a minute than I thought they would be. That was the
dream, did I mention you lived down the street but not printing?
   In panicles, now what's his name's been here, Yellowstone National
Park, and in some involuntary and faithless way he wound up insulting
us, it was as if he didn't notice or know any better though, not consoli-
dated. Women in the armed forces, well there was something about di-

98

visiveness as if to achieve the gathered material like a rose or pleat among the senses of power, cactus, even the prickly pear type but I've no sense of what it was but I've had it with the Nobel Prizes and Virgin Mary being a bad friend, any of a number of related trees and hideous acquaintances like Antoine de Cadillac and the aforementioned Mary making me nervous for no real reason for centuries, after all cement fastens things together, it's a smooth-skinned fruit like the way so-and-so played ball, great with great spirit, so did she and she did too and she also did in a circle like a Congreve match or else it was pointless. Gulf of Mexico, family life is so crowded in exile, we're broke too and every day is a fast clock but no news of the time or even of small size manages to come except archaic, I've gotta get back to normal thinking so I can do some probability towards the exile like a cactus to plan ahead or write but I can't till I find out where to throw out a fly like in fishing or being stung on the head by a bee in dreaming, certainly not no more teaching, I'm hoping there's nothing to teach, pointless printing of a small size like a clock that's fast or the old-fashioned Congreve match, I hope I'm not pregnant again. I'm sure all the gathered material and money will be in the mail tomorrow like you-know-who's anguish and I don't blame him I know exactly what he means except that his feelings somehow seem more genuine in panicles like the wheat or oat plant than mine which don't do that, gone fishing but I'll know tomorrow though I feel more than of a small size and love to work out like an atomic clock at softball or something but there's no use doing anything else till I find out I guess.

You always say something all of a sudden I didn't know you'd noticed since there are so many ways in which I feel I know you better than I really do know you like that guy quoting that thing he quoted by guess who about sex. I mean about coming I was thinking of writing but first what I was talking about when I said that was Marie's teeth and the way you described them. Like taking the sense out of normal talking but it too is worn down or worn out so everything that's left is new like the idea of moving to New Orleans near the Gulf of Mexico like an exile just for fun though and the plural impassivity of seeing all new things but racism, you say maybe that's a superficial archaic printing do you think I mean the town might be as justly quaint like the craving for a smooth-skinned fruit as this place is or someplace even worse than this maybe, it's taking a pitted chance, I forgot to say it also has a smooth pit too. Alot of them never do anything at all so why do we have them? I mean are we attracted to the exile of love and from even motion? Then with the gathered material using alot of run-on dependent clauses in the archaic cities and not printing the towns like they do, we will go except I can't make them up they have to just happen because I can't get to remember what they even are, do you know what I mean, but if you point one out to me, and this is like the zoo, then I'll be able to name it instantly, is it Fool's Parsley or Poison Hemlock or just a wild carrot, commonly called Queen Anne's Lace? Nobody seemed to even want to think about it, then I thought vinegar, remember we mentioned it instead of using expensive lemons, still no money had come don't forget, I could do a book that would have that kind of friction Congreve invented in it, it would be designed with a structure the way I heard somebody talking about a Lincoln Continental but this would just be for mimeographing and rather than being related to money in any way it would be like the way she said that they were the kinds of things people said after they saw them, I'm astonished, I'm a changed person, it's amazing, you see it was a ritual kept secretly and only shown or open to I don't know who. But I think I mentioned those Eleusinian mysteries before didn't I? It wasn't the same Congreve by the way who wrote comedies of manners who did the match but they did have the same name, William, and the inventor did a rocket too. I won't mention that I wanted to mention, and not to one Congreve or which one, the idea of forgetting the loss of beauty without anger just to have some fun and not be so moralistic about it but it didn't matter anyway because I know you can guess who had this to say which is sort of why bother.

Then after I thought of the dream and I saw the older unexpected rooms in it more like instinct or the bee sting thing to be like a penis and so on, this pipe got too hot, it was the small one and I couldn't even finish the normal pipeful, it's like remembering a story I was telling "him" while we were walking across the grass, remember that day we had all played ball for a while, remember we found some kind of kitchen knife in the grass, I can't remember what the story was though, it had something to do with evil, oh it was about t.v. and shooting up heroin & about a brand new car, then it seemed like there would have to be some explaining to do because of my funny manner because I shouted and sounded all of a sudden like I was talking but still on the streets of Brooklyn and then I remember this story about "her" and it was she bought her father a new car, something really fancy, but then who said she wasn't going to or what was to stop her, or, what do they say, who ever thought otherwise?

In the sweet grass of the fast night's clock which I know is still there like a craving to get as high as some other time you can't even be sure you didn't remember wrong, when I think that I always think it's exactly like childhood, this was some experiment to see what would happen to the words, it's all so fucking ephemeral or steams or smokes in some way or else what I mean is sensational in the sensational sense except you can't help seeing I won't say it's all just talk. 1979-80.

And I didn't want to say either or nor did I want to mention by way of introduction that those words just walked or sauntered in, worse chance than having a guest who perhaps drinks all the beer very fast and then puts the wine you've been saving for dinner on the table for everyone to share on Sunday when you can't get any more. It's terrible to be broke and have no words from the beer and to run around as fast as you can and find the words that happened to come in have only introduced you back into exile from which you write letters harping about the truth having learned to speak at all from elucidating the mess of a certain house by mail to the landlady, and from describing babies, I don't know if you know what I'm talking about, I think it was because one of us didn't have it in him or her just that afternoon, see you soon.

THE FLY HAS MARRIED THE BUMBLE BEE

There's always something to be said for some kind of nothing like having nothing on the other side though it might not be economic, there are millions of things you and I don't know about, did one or the other of the ones who wrote what has not been written for us to read think that. Something about the sun being so hot it hurts your face but then you say to me you are being so sensitive you cannot even eat for fear your desk is on fire at home but it's cold at night like it's supposed to be but never is. Why waste it on something that doesn't make any money she said but I had hardly ever thought that way, you are brooding. Your vacation sounded good even with the car. This painting of a woman is overwhelming and romantic, it confuses me like these alternating moods. Friendly enemies have been struggling to get watchdogs and money which they call the long green. It's amazing that the sun went down then as if we had even come close to uniform identification like sisters, yes or no. And then somebody had the nerve to say hang on as if each paragraph was about a different subject. He's the kind of person who makes jokes about my name that remind me of someone devoted to Max Beerbohm, or anybody's name for that matter. It must seem weird to other people for us to do anything the way we do it like the ocean is stormy whether it is or not. She told me she liked babies but the rest of the kinds of people were all fucked up but she didn't say fucked up, she said something else that was rather more architectonic and textile than musical. In high school when we learned new big words we took them one at a time and were supposed to use them in conversation three times so we wouldn't forget what they meant, I feel so crazy, someone said the good weather was making us all sleepy, someone else said maybe it's because you're pregnant but then it could be promise and just laws. One girl is "it," she is given both ropes. It said you capitalist company will make money if you are honest and patient. I can't forget the girl with the candy pacifier who hooted at the boy in the see-through shirt by our house or the shell-shocked veteran who dressed up as a policeman with a policeman's hat and a shirt that said "Security Officer." Like these moods I can't figure out if I want to be bordered with remembering. He said you couldn't write criticism anymore because no one was objective, I can't remember why but it made sense at the time, now it sounds like nothing. The night passes but there's still a little light in the sky, certainly he would never dream of writing novels. I gave the impression of being strong but I will tell you about the *picus-nicus,* that was how they began to try to teach us Latin, I'll never forget it. I couldn't figure out if anything should be done but I couldn't do nothing as if someone was ordering me to furnish the room, find the possum, know your town, pass the fox. I was at the Greek Olympic Ball when I saw I would have to focus more on one thing, I am a tree. Those blue clouds will soon be black for hunger and the earth is pink for fun. The foodstamp people wouldn't be too happy if there were beer stains on the rent egret, I think marriage is designed to make you detailed enough for love but that love is different. She told me about the young woman whose hair turned white because of her ovaries, it reminded me of the pregnant woman telling me about the other pregnant woman who didn't see the doctor at all as I'd planned not to but then suddenly she found out she had a dread disease anyway. I won't tell you what it was, you see I could never say this in poetry, there is a difference to be told. Did I just want to take it easy like spin the bottle or the wit and wisdom of good Pope John or was I hoping to make something of my summer vacation yet I can't go home after that or it might be the frightening idea of having to tell my autobiography with all the steps between absorption and reaction as if life was an allergy. I had formed the first sentence in my sleep until I remembered hearing someone saying she was reading the novels of George Sand and they were wonderful. As every poem had become the same length so every sentence was beginning to end the same like taxicab. She told me why she was unhappy, shall I now tell you? So far we know a number of people who live around here who have to have two cars, that seems inedible to me, the other car would be strawberries, crabmeat, wine, not to speak of all the idiotic delicacies you can read about in the papers. The main car, it's the big one, it's the man's car sometimes, the first car, it's meat. Hideous meat with all its sluggish qualities, dead meat unlike the pleasures of squalid sex or a woman listening to somebody saying it's nine months of pain, one moment of pleasure (Simone de Beauvoir) or the cultivation of sadism for an art we all know about, I know the existence of another person has little to do with jogging in the sense that the women who love babies without realism foster the idealism of the absence of meat in our lives. So I have to say with her white teeth will be whorled before us for love. How the ram's head lady's slipper got along with the male sleepy catchfly when they were in bed too is beyond us. Each smooth phlox like the wild sweet william is like I could rather say who each flower was like, I'll be then the pearly everlasting fool's parsley and you can be the wild cucumber they call a balsam apple but that it makes us not a family, my yellow vetchling. We had a list of games and names of automatic plays of flowers to stay our later love, you mentioned you had walked in this chaotic absent space that's covered here and I couldn't help but do what you were doing. In order to tell you I will rearrange the house but it's not a house. Left alone it's just an ousted flower I have to iron like a long poem written by Philip Whalen in script that could then be rolled up and placed in a tube. Or if it wasn't a tube what could it be? We aren't even sure we want all this continuing on with all there is to notice. So I'm afraid that is just how I'm feeling, like a zigzag relay, tomorrow I'll have another pregnancy test too and it's to be given in the king's English so that *How To Write* will become a Modern Herbal and if the book I write in becomes a dictionary I'll be embarrassed to have said that I had seen myself this way, like the young woman in the picture, the huge spider with eight legs and two small forelegs who is sitting on this page with the tenacity of a love I cannot stop watching for fear it will fall on my leg.

I wish I was twenty again because of the accuracy then of knowing what to do next whereas now I'm put in the place of the woman who looks like me who has to say I think I know more than you do, Doctor, but I am frightened and I too have presented a false picture, so I understand you. As we lose our beauty do you speak from memory or must I pretend to be as young but old as all the time that's seemed to pass would make me which I am. Do you know this flower, why can't I consult you, I was wondering if it was hemlock and what kind? Rosemary picked the bladder campions I had called St. Johnswort. Boy it is impossible to tell most of them one from the other but for the bean sprouts when they look like Indian Pipe and the pretty Swamp Saxifrage. How come I don't have nobody to tell me if it's Featherbells or not, we belong in this word puzzle. This guy or that, our ideal men, never got us out of it, I don't mean nothing against men by that, I don't not mean it. I just meant this particular writer, a you know who, without any meaning, you get my message he was more than clear about everything. More than Roger Tory Peterson or someone. You see there are families of flowers and despite my own dispute with them I find what you are saying about families being all wrong all wrong, you say the family is a star or a commonplace bill; to be sure it is that general shape or structure with distinctions between the species. I am keyed to see the absoluteness of the will in brief and non-technical descriptions of all the families. Yet it's true, unlike conventional arrangements, you can view the whole by flipping the pages as of a book, you get a visual impression including color. Who will identify this system? Is a man or woman to be predictable yet again, even while the nitwitted church bells are still ringing where you or I am? The bells are not women, they are not built or woven, heavy metal things hanging there, nowadays recorded, not even rung by the rope like a poem still read without a lyric instruction. Numbers cultivate the extremities of will until I die because I wore my hair like a curtain and you saw nothing at all. They said she had no curtains but hung cases of showy flowers and frightening herbs in her windows, she took deadly poisons into her house because they grew omnivorously, her sister said she'd learned to expect to study them and take them in like beggars, no one could visit anyway because they had no money. She was the ultimate doctor's daughter, the landlord was afraid to breathe in her presence. I know chicory is blue and alien like the white wild chamomile. I would hope to be able to pay your bill soon if I were tall as this year's goldenrod. I cannot have another, I am a heart passed. Miss Daisy Fleabane

CLARK COOLIDGE

FROM: COMES THROUGH IN THE CALL HOLD
(Improvisations on Cecil Taylor)

Wait, wristless, wisdoms
a warmer thing waltzes
slim and then over the thing, abatement
rolled and summed and turning I see it
art is late
higher things
grown old grown list
parting of all this imitate brought over the thing in mass
paper parting gone valve and the sold
fleeting are the olds dawn involves tipping seen
bound and in case, the dulls encase emerge
long of light and trait of sunk, the bread
it's a large bound bold stapling and mounted
larging leaver toldening the bulge encarrots
brown lip to lunge and ate at
cars selling various get paid to
set right at hand the valve lights
longer thing in timorous odd
dream weights, slow shadow mating you
all this is popular, dated, caustic paradise
got
a snow came, his part in things a crow
things it couldn't be you remember
I am the great seller, going thrown sand flue
and goneness is my name, rights to be endless
even to be careful and best the fuels away large dad
coils, hills, told, various, breaks, flanagan

I come right home to the horn you sell peculiar
shows

All floats cow the mines back to fruity barrier
is it said to be the capsules silence carmine?
all goes into and threat later a spark higher
tuner lets its belt when you are you are
car gets turner and he threads and height weights
spelling won't get you through, whelm you
going past it writing the end of pall spells
gone the going part, going the rights of threat
your clothing, do you have a weather?
are you careful to better catch
the right winner way your form of women
silking the struck icer in and no pretenser
the magic coils off in such housing winning
you got flavors? the fire is able to
ball whelks catching at walls of the flame
carting it flowers?   dreaming down here counts
and dams?   ovular ounce of window
trend is to, gots it, bets once and never
again I'm dunce, you've said, priced
so lucky to win at sandwich, price list, stew
brighter lessons gone on to hook here the palaces
the entreaty mindlessness when
but, pleater character gets, the more
it's such that sun drops, then drains, then
cauliflower, rhisomes, enclitic rag
loudness next to a sun, barrier cats forming
back it comes carefuller, read the bread's book
part of this is carrier, later the snatch will break
and, no one knows the newling trapped inside
cart hoards matching and capturing, the man stores
I can be caught out crabbing, maturing sister

do you count?   rised in lumps and court
over by the far factory, tongues, limp, strew
particle twilight, untrue light, coughing wakeful
but he ends doesn't end goes right through to end
shoves his pants ends into the sound sphere
spearing pennies, speaking of cash, ending against a wall
of told tones, lemons in hand and carrying stone
I live and oh no the sound is past capturing
one wall gives then the next, the calm, the
overdone helm of raising you hadn't had
in fact weren't the facts at all your mom
and I pick up the glancing device and startle
and your home is gone with starers
and the valve is a hand I couldn't do
outside of the spare withouts you cashed
worn it wristed then and throat comes
the light cans

VICTOR HERNÁNDEZ CRUZ

FROM: **THREE MOVEMENTS**

AFRICA_ Choreo Thoughts

The mother of metaphor
For sound is deciphered to
Specific meaning
Nature is made to obey
The rhythm of a voice
Or the hands upon a drum
Within a prior consent
of the cosmos
The man and woman that knows
the alphabet
Can speak the letters
It is a way of being
That stayed strongly itself
within the Catholics Hispanas
It can change shapes and names
while the inside stays the same

AFRICA IS CALLING ME LIFTING UP MY FEET

The holy rhythm
The rhythmic soul of the Caribbean

THE CONGA IS A TELEPHONE
R I N G
BOMA PU TA KA TA BUUM
BOMBA PU TA KA TA BUUM

From New Orleans
To Tango land
IN Vera Cruz and Ecuador
In Cartagena and Lima Peru
Africa has in each place a home

INDIO AFRO HISPANO
Along Andalusian Spanish
In Chicago San Francisco and
New York
We carry a treasure within
to cherish and preserve
But most important to EXPRESS.

ESPAÑA SPAIN

Conquer-conquere conquist
Inquisition
Conquering conquist
Allah chased the visigoths
to the Pyrennees
Where for 800 years they
stared at rocks
Fans of knowledge opened
in Cordova   Grenada
There was peace and discourse
Some visigoths came back
and learned
Medicine and how to play guitar

HISPANIA
Falling into Africa
of the North
Now too your eyes are

dark
And your hands walk upon
strings
I say that you are also a door
Cultural spirits go in and out
Flavors reach their destinations
Whole bodies were stolen by
Gypsies and made to dance

Andalusia
The earth of which
Harvests poets
Who are given words by
fervent   souls
Describing settings not here yet
"The eye cannot see the essential things"

Out of the blue they came
To where the sea shells made echoes
Things have never been the same

ESPAÑA   CONQUEST   CONQURE
Conquering
Hispania the hidden will now
arise
With red clay on its face.

THE COCONUT CLOCK

By spacing the counted moments of
appearance as it presents itself in
Places
By celestial planification
We happened both at the post office

———

line.
Sending mail and boxes off to different
infinities
Specific Caribees—
Her wonder made her play with her
hair
The vein of love riding through
the juices of the nerves
Despite herself she flies
For that very reason I have become
Space

The air is a radio transmitting
as if surprised at surprised
Somewhere inside that vision is
a group of numbers adding up.
Shy to rise her eyes directly
As her fingers no longer hers
Whirlpool endless black curls,

Her features
Migration Catalan infused with
Caribbean tribes
Her nose the superior of the blend
Nostralgia native
Pride installed in flesh
A yellow with a spray of red

A painting of a first orgasm
Appears in memorial fountain
Her face blushes rushes rosy
A journey from the tinge of papaya
That has shifted into hazel nut

As the rooster and chicken leave
the small tile of encounter,
At the post office
The correspondence goes off.

GOOD WATERS

We do not claim to be of the fallen
The tradition of Aqueybana was not
Just within the material
It was not just in the people physical
In rhythm it was what still dances
In gene Plazas
Orbiters of extraction
Luminers of the messages in songs
The laws of travel
The events of the trajectory
How we formed in the interior
The round bohios
Which became the shape of our
Transmitting dance
Back home-shakers of maracas

Do not talk of things that do not
exist
The presence is the presence
Claim for good the good of the good
Now claim you the delicious of the
Delight you gain
From the lost of the good to the
Out of step
And what out of goodness it was
That now the horizon vegetation

Chokes and the coming progression
Has no water or air
The tradition wanted more good for
The good to distribute throughout
Without finishing the spot—
It knew that beyond the needs there
Was no need   to progress into that
Uptempo pace impossible to dance
That's the "one voice to call back
the good of the good we have lost"

Even such that comes to your tongue
That too is there
No matter what or where
Aca or Alla
For conflict nuts
Say : Adjuntas and Chicago

We do not claim to be of the fallen
We are still delivering sound in red packages
Upon this there was only an attempt
At something happening
At the edge of realization
We are still waiting
We have not fallen.

GO-BETWEEN BETWEEN

Language does more than merely communicate and "express." It arrives, it manifests, it is a relationship. We are all languages. Are language and culture really opposed, are speech & writing opposed, what's the "dialogue" between langue & parole? What does this mean / "matter to" the poet? Does a text truly exist outside the world? How is "speech" inside the world? Do these questions come out of my western tradition, a tradition narrow in scope &, finally, irritating? I am personally interested, in my own writing & in the writing of others, how the writing *sounds* in the world. How the writing initiates itself as sound first, how it resonates in my body. How it seems to move from heart to *hara* to mouth. How I perceive this reading others' text on the page silently, how the poets I pay attention to mouth "it." I am interested in the psychological states the "writing" activates & provokes, and how I might sound three different "voices" of these states. How the writing is a kind of go-between between states of mind (heart, body) hidden & states of mind realized, enacted as well as what's overheard. I wish always to pursue this relationship and push the experience beyond the page. Yet honoring the page. Page which is shapely, literate, which originates as a kind of cosmic void. What hope & fear exists facing the blank white page? Does the computer change this stark joy? I am afraid of getting lost inside the machine, another kind of fear. I get up & dance when I can't sit still. I mouth the syllables. I play with the words. I play on the cosmic battlefield of the blank page and of the room's silence, for writing is a kind of war. And yet I take the words where I can get them.

In the Thai tradition, to interpret a text in a reading or performance is to "ti bot"—*to strike the text,* much the way you would sound or strike a musical gong. In my travels to Asia (particularly to various parts of India, Nepal and Bali) and in my own ongoing study & practice of Tibetan Buddhism, I've experienced that the sounding of the words has an intrinsic power. That the word exists to both vibrate "out of" and also to enter the psycho-physical system as well as the larger environment (it's all inter-connected). That seed syllables travel and carry certain efficacies. I heard two Vedic masters chanting for hours from the *Rig Veda* at a festival in Bhopal several years ago. They had been trained in this classical tradition since childhood. They were essentially priests of the texts, holders of the texts, and vessels for the wisdom and power of the texts. Yet each of them had a distinct, you could say almost a "personal" style, and they were both *living* the Veda. Thus the audience was receiving a direct "hit" or transmission of the text through both the refinement of tradition as well as the immediate call to have it come alive, be actualized in performance. This performance contrasted with the appearance of the Bauls of Bengal, singers as well as dancers, during the same festival. The three Baul performers work within a less refined yet more spontaneous street tradition. The music has secular appeal, a sensual appeal. It's demonstrative, vibrant. They were dressed colorfully, with an androgynous aspect to their garb & gesture, in marked contrast to the pristine white-robed Vedic masters. And yet at root both performances shared the premise of hitting the text, striking the form to achieve a kind of holy synchronized ecstasy. Both traditions exhibit highly evolved and subtle manifestations of "siddhi" (sacred energy or knowledge).

The literature known as Old Javanese (9th century A.D., Java) has many poems written in the tradition of Sanskrit literature drawing on both Sanskrit and Javanese vocabularies. Each poem begins with a *manggala* or invocation that establishes the poet's understanding between him/her self, the text & the world. A text called the "Sumanasan-taka" begins by invoking the god of beauty *(Lango)* who is concealed in the dust of the pencil sharpened by the poet. Lango is asked to descend into the letters of the poem as if they were his temple. The god is not an external deity or savior in the theistic sense, but rather a refined consciousness or sensibility—not "of" the relative world of the senses.

Through this deity one breaks through dualistic illusion to meet reality, as it is, face to face. Without veils. Lango literally means "enraptured." Langa joins "man" and nature together. So the deity is a kind of vehicle for realization of *things as they are.* This is a principle in the practices of Tibetan Buddhism as well. One invokes the yidams or deities as manifestations of more awakened states of mind (energy without ego is the idea here), invites them to descend and unites with them. Haiku traditionally also works with this heaven–earth–man principle. Man, the concrete image in the haiku, is what joins heaven & earth. Lango is similar to the Sanskrit "rasa." (Sanskrit poetry/poetics has its origins in the Vedic hymns circa 1,500 B.C.) Rasa literally meant liquid, sap, semen, but later became "the essence of a thing." According to Sanskrit poetics, the poet traditionally needed to possess "Vyutpatti"—vast knowledge of the world (culture), "Abyhasa"—a skill with language developed from constant practice and apprenticeship with a master, and "Sakti," creative power. Sakti relates to the sounding of the text. Mantra, in the Buddhist sense, is explained as that which protects the cohesiveness of the "vajra mind." "Vajra" is the quality of clarity, indestructibility. The Vajra mind is diamond-like, "beyond arising and ceasing." Mantra is a means of transforming energy through sound, expressed by speech, breathing and movement. Mantras are Sanskrit words or syllables and express the synchronized quintessence of the various energies with or without conceptual meaning. From a certain point of view, the Buddhist practitioner recognizes all sound as mantra. From this poet's "absolute" point of view, all sound as poetry.

In a recent trip to Bali I was aware again and again of the intrinsic power of words and how they are included as necessary parts of ritual activity, especially in the long *wayang kuilt* (shadow puppet) performances. How as the *dalang* (priest-puppeteer) moves the languages around (Kawi, high & low Balinese and Bahasa Indonesia, the *lingua franca* of Indonesia) while all the realms, actual & psychological, are being invoked. He or she mouths many different voices which are literal extracts of *The Ramayana* & *The Mahabharata* as well as spontaneous improvised comic banter. This *wayang* is a prescribed enactment, still the most popular form of ritual entertainment in Bali. It resonates with all ages and experience and may be heard on many levels: dream, history, battleground, personality, religion, pure sound & vision (the shadows are mere illusions on the screen). The idea of "ti bot" is highly evolved in this kind of performance. Language as such is more than a predictable medium of communication, here more than a mere system of signs, for it plays an ongoing role in the process of "imagining and interpreting" the world.

There's a patterning in my own nervous system which I enjoy & respect & manifest in my own writing & in the performance of my writing, & which resonates with other patterns in the world. The describer, the artist, is always a person. We need these present eyeballs and ears & bodies to register "our world" as it flies. Every syllable is conscious. On and off the page. I am not interested in distancing the "audience" (myself) from the text, from the enactment of text. Thought & language are metabolically linked and this psycho-physical system is also open to any pulses that arise. These typing fingers are transmitters.

I recently put together BOOK I (fourteen sections) of the long poem, IOVIS OMNIA PLENA, the "tribute / ritual enactment / hag's rage" on the theme of male energy. On another level it simply delights in many voices as the *wayang kulit* does. Both high and low, ecclesiastical and vernacular. I am writing this poem, for it continues, as survival. It performs itself in me as I read it aloud and it establishes the relationship to the constant challenge of masculine "siddhi" as a kind of syllabic balance. The Lango of the poem is the thematic semen. I wrote the *Manggala* after compiling BOOK I (200 pages) & it came as a kind of prayer-psalm, & calls up the Biblical messiah. The last pages of BOOK I (Section 14) conjure the Qu'ran, an old Cary Grant movie, a conversation with ten-year-olds, a "take" on *Five Easy Pieces* from Clark Coolidge, and a Sanskrit invocation to "one-pointedness."

FROM: IOVIS OMNIA PLENA

a gap in my life . . .

I was a mutant, but . . .

a gold tooth in my mouth proclaiming

a gap in my life, but . . .

Yet silhouette of a High Priestess my own mind was too . . .

Mosaic too, I was a reminder, but . . .

The hair of a pearl in my heart

or memory of Keats' tomb in Rome

But, is texture true? But? Is it?

I had a memory toward the Editorial Board

whose life attitudes were not sound

& Yeats' burial place (ah dear dead poets)

I worshiped all of them, diamonds, opals, guns . . .

Picture a distributor cap with pinions stuck out

Feels good in my hand

in the chaos of my life

Feels good in any laboratory of desire

& back in the hand, holding the reins of desire

I was a truant, but . . .

– Dead guts & bones sticking out of the sand, that's war.

– Blood & bullets flying through the air.

– Michael J. Fox is in casualties.

– Tom Cruise is born on the 4th of July.

– Explosions ah dead, everybody gone now.

– The world is nothing.

– A Stealth blows up the enemy base.

– M-16 machine guns down whatever in sight.

– Iraq has as many tanks as both sides of World War II.

– They fight over who's going to be the President of a dollar bill.

– So what is a thrill, boys?

– Hitting a home run, a grand slam.

– Swearing at the Sega. I cuss at Wonder Boy, whatever he does.

– You cuss at the game because it cheated & a guy killed you or a bad snake or a mushroom or a snail or a fish killed you

– They waste yr butt on Mega Man II.

– If you're Metal Man in Mega Man II you can blow their guts right out of their shells.

– Winning is pretty fun.

– Feels weird. "Hand–eye coordination," all that.

– This is easy. Look, look. I'm trying to turn.

– I got 11 on Aztec Adventure.

– Winning Bubble Bobble at level #24.

– " God damn you Tommy Lasorda"

(I take that back)

Telling the story

telling the story on the hour

How to become a writer out of the rib of a man

How to spit out the man's marrow to breathe free

How to stand on the ground & contend with articulate hormones

How not to get sick in the midnight hour

(Give me a break!)

Oh, and the last movie character I recall identifying strongly with, and it amazed me as I hadn't had this sort of experience in a long while, was the Bobby Dupea character Jack Nicholson played in Five Easy Pieces. Especially that scene where he's goaded into playing that Chopin étude by the Susan Anspach character and the camera goes around the walls of the room, you see his whole life in those family pictures, then the piece ends and she tells him it was lovely and she really felt something and he says he just picked the easiest piece he could remember and felt nothing at all himself. Of course, I come from a similar musical background, but I think it was more the sexual tension mixed up with a misreading of art in that scene I felt I knew from the inside. From then on I felt I knew his thoughts, and this seldom happens to me with movies. More often I feel like I can read the director's thoughts.

kauśalya-ekagrata-citta

References:

Stephen Lansing, *The Three Worlds of Bali*
Notes from Andrew Schelling workshop, The Naropa Institute, 1989

BRUCE ANDREWS

BEYOND SUTURE

LET THE VERB BE 'REOPEN'—'REORDER'*

Poetry is redemption from pessimism.—All lendings off, meaning utterly unsafe,—athwart and sundered—flickers in the rigging—F r a g m e n t s   o f   a   L i q u i d a t i o n—to be read by guesswork through obliteration

LET MINUS ONE BE PLUS ONE

We are a small remnant // of signal escapes wonderful in themselves—Identities and configurations rupture and shift.—she escapes the violence of definition,—*Formation of a Separatist*—Who knows // what number in number alone / stands heretic // if one is not—Ego vanished and—Am in a simple allegory // Reaching out alone in words oh // peerless poesy—An executant enunciates multiplicity.—We are too finite—

I LOST PERSPECTIVE

ReddenBorderViewHaloPast ApparitionOpenMostNotion *is*—tracing points – vertices – stages—Confusion // of lines bisecting   shred—I pick my compass to pieces—Well structure could fall / Preys troop free—asquint / askew—sh   dispel   iris   sh—

THE FIX IS OFF

Transgression links . . . / Dark spell—invisible / inviolable—Outside the window fictions are / crumbling—Lines surrender occult adieu // Negation coils its coldest constellation—*My map is rotten and frayed—*

LANGUAGE MAKES MORE GAPS

The Perfectibilitarians were wrong—the little heir of alphabet / lean as a knife / searches . . . in tatters—healingly into a depth—in syllables caesura—must always undo or sever—For we are language   Lost / in language— refuses / to be comforted // because they *are* not.—Her instinctive one-sided discourse abolishes one-sidedness. —The stream bisects the stage.—But in writing Language advances into remembering that there is no answer imagining Desire.—Know the combustible dark—Stammer.—I have imagined a center // Wilder than this region / The figment of a book // Scarce broken letters—pivot bravura—Irruptives—*unfocused future*—

STARRY NIGHTS WITHOUT A SELF-SUFFICING LEXICON

—intimacy with Vacancy was Expanse, not Truth.—Witnesses are all humans linking or heralding truth or transgression in a grammatical irruption of grace abounding.—Face answers to face / limit and quiet Limit // Field of vision and field of future—Face to fringe of itself / foreseen form from far off—The doors of the fortress are open—horizons wandering   real world—Not a trace. We are at peace – pathless— Nameless abashing flame.—I might withdraw into distance beyond name.—In distant discourse I trace a Stranger self.—darkened by outstripped possession / Field stretching out of the world—a rupture into contraries.—Gun stays awake guarding the Distance.—

THE SOCIAL: PARADE REST . . . ATTENTION . . .
ABOUT FACE . . . LEFT FACE

Physiognomy of Liberty—quintessential clarity of inarticulation—everything possible—in Contradiction's originary ebullience, an end to passive consumerism.—Our masters re-interpreted as monsters—in a land of pages // where the No's have it—The expanse of unconcealment / so different from all maps—only Mutability certain.—between rupture and rapture—Counterjudgment—Clamor in the theatre of alienation.—Hoop // of horizon / negation pursuit and illusion—splitting nature's shadow / splitting the world

---

* Indented paragraphs are made up of phrases, separated by long dashes, from Susan Howe's works: *Articulation of Sound Forms in Time*—'The Captivity and Restoration of Mrs. Mary Rowlandson—*Defenestration of Prague*—'Federalist 10'—'Heliopathy'—*The Liberties*—*My Emily Dickinson*—*Pythagorean Silence*—*Secret History of the Dividing Line*—'Thorow'—'Women and Their Effect in the Distance'

PULSED SCALE

(Abigail Child, *Climate/Plus,* Coincidence Press, Oakland, 1986)

"How are we today?" Managed, administered to be a job without recall. Majority for war's not forgiven, equivocal center in flashes to pass, signalled into silence. Control is framed all over silhouetting connectedness with optical uncertainty. Speech, artificial intelligence dreaming the exceptions to well-being weight straightens out function. Phonemes are pressure jamming flesh defection; hybridize edge, impeachable. Exemplary deviance a defect (ticket shots)—artificial flesh in succession unacceptable units inside equivalence. Machine content tracks the slippage. Phantasy property enthusiasm break off, apologist: novice = copy, uncontradicted pronoun, limits plummeting. Tool error. Ideological unflooding, formless impedance—conceit equally misinterpreting serial ads ikon undressed, archlights to victim. Movement non-exclusive; go for it, in context. Affabilities dismantle impediment, serial, disconcerted dispersal unparalleled eponymous clients. Forfeit repetition. Infatuation echoes disarm critique, language of interest involuntaries. Globed & shaped resistible—frontiers beside attention paratactic breeding, matrix wobbly intrinsic (noise) capacity's magnificence proliferates. In fissures scale particularizes—social ensemble breaks over struggle's light. Commodity ballast one of a kind impasse bent over independence backing up utility of measures is meaning powerless space. Demythologized impetuosity this time, of equality heightens writing . . . sense resembles writing. Rhythm adjudicates, 'high face' slave to prove it less privatized, intrinsic defies degree curve valorize release: pluralization not anonymous, too typical factions obscure the negatives licensed for needs "(during the war.)"

white adhocism

white adolescent

white attribution

white bed

white claimant

white disruptions

white era

white fungible

white giveaways

white hour

white I

white jerk

white kelvinator

white less

white matter

white no

white out

white prearrangment

white quiescence

white rap

white stupidity

white *tipico*

white [unintelligible]

white vote

white who

white xerox

white yanking

white zeitgeist

IN THE FLESH

I.

Billy giving them just enough light — naked on a bench inflated — he's got sleepless night — dancing in his mind showering waiting for glimpses — it's so big down here. "Relax," Coach said like melting, some spit from one corner of his mouth — through the window as the freshman — "keep your voice from getting carried away while we're still schoolboys."

As he combed his hair — the comb through his hair — glassy eyes rubbing — the look in his eyes splashing . . .

Billy — pink — his pink towel — pink legs outstretched — split open and force his mouth — from his rural home to the highway rest-stop, drink. His most serious dad — suspect what he was doing — trembled in the stomach — Billy running down white porcelain, photographing. "What're you doing in there?" "I think I gotta shit."

In the leather easy chair — autumn on the back yard — shapes created by a fire — on the thick carpeting, "Dad?" — hesitation — "Do I have to go with all those other guys in the woods?" The kid was changing, because the kid looked worshipful — when he didn't have to — gazed at his barefooted — small, on the other hand, defined — sometimes gruff with the boy — trying to calm his breathing had shook him up — his own or the boy's? — whose renegade twinge some late evening has been rebuilt in each bedroom, larger than kingsize.

Out of the corner of his eye Billy was looking, Billy could smell — it was himself from where he stood, his own in response — had to quickly found himself — get a move on — with his own definite tension restlessly in their denser secluded faces. . .

As if he'd been hit with a cream pie — up in the air down his throat — I wanna believe the words — an explosion in the sunny spot — aimed at a human being this time as if seeing him for the first time — letting himself be another boy, the two boys, some kind of son doing down there — unable to say the words off his forehead — loud in the still air.

Billy gasped, nearly purple — holding hands for support — glanced at each other — they both fell several times — searched frantically for the moment and began to lick the wounds.

His back, his front, his body out long — what I am doing would never recover — just acting, not thinking — pressed into one smooth motion rolled back his life. No man had ever — his father's mouth — never enough tongue — turned back into his blue eyes, wider than before. His lips shuddered throughout his body. "Billy" — into Billy — he clung to the man — "How does it feel to be a mouth?"

II.

An entire summer with my dead mother's brother's sons: I could hardly wait! They go to church in the fields; I want to be in there with them. I flexed, I soaped — corn silk — I would unfold each new adventure of each new day. My cousins' suntans.

I shook hands with all-knowing uncle — corn on the cob, blackberry cobbler — unpack — they watched me — wanting and doing his scattered brown hair down your spine. I remembered summers sleeping — that praise — in the stable with the horses and the milking machine.

Atop the clean white sheets watching each other — length and size — sleep tight in the breeze each form breathing to claim our veins, channels . . . "Are you asleep yet?" "I can't sleep."

I like that.

We traded kisses to experiment heartbeats. His body flew to my mouth — he was trying to keep from screaming — exploding the snowy sheets in the dark nests of his sweetness — he — doing as I had done — pulling his breath into his knees in a rush of white.

"Is that the lesson for today?"

"No, this is. . ."

III.

Jimmy was cute; he buried his face in socks. He picked up one of the school jerseys and gazed at the sight of himself. He lifted wet fingers and achieved sensations. Watching himself he was watching himself.

A guy wearing a guy over his nose — sweaty eggs — he inhaled peppery flanks, wiggled his toes. He swayed — streaming thought in the world — drunk against his unbelievable fingers — superman rain — strained to hold himself still. Football practice was finished.

Hal stood facing him, gym bag in hand. You know how it is: a man lays down.

"I won't say a word" — don't say another word — he studied, stepped back, didn't move, sit up, got up, started to, go ahead, I guess so, I hope so, turned toward Jimmy, the distant and romantic past.

He leaned down his soft legs — sheen of shower soap — beads of a necklace — down on your animal hands and knees — shiver through conflicting orders   thrilled at being a clear pearl — planted on the floor.

Jimmy watched Hal leaned over, tangled his eyes, jockey briefs on the door knob, of his neck pulling slowly by the hair up toward — and turned every muscle in his body to perfumed oil, filling the air.

The long lines of his high back closed around his hips. His nipples were bubbling under the cobra heart. Radiation all over the floor. He could actually hear energy — scalp sizzled — their breaths slumped over them, expressionless.

Absent-minded sweaty face. He looked down at himself. Now I finish my shower. Now I see your face again. Now I leave this place — whirled — waiting for the sounds of Hal's leaving — distant sound of the locker-room door. Now I can't sit down.

Cove high school at the top of the blossoming hill. The sky stood looking — making it autumn — late afternoon — a state of euphoria in the laundry room — watching them in silence — hovered and flushed with heat — from the row of lockers after school had closed. Jimmy in the air — waiting for something — I'm one of you — another knot in his throat.

IV.

He could do it. It's all right. Jason in his arms. "Thanks, Dad, but I'm all right." At arms length — "I care alot" — unbuttoned his shirt — "I'll show you" — pulled off his socks — "how much I" — hugged together — "care."

"You, too!" He could hardly stand up — buried his nose in disbelief, disappeared into his son's mouth.

Jason was panting — my skin — the boy — my Dad — out of him — inside his body. Rhythmically deeper — perfectly vertical inside — to the level of both their heads — Jason's room lit by the streetlight, hunkered down in the moonlight, pouring his lips over another world, distant, deep, content.

He felt such terror against the side of the mattress. The boy lay before him, wrapped with relief. He was doing a darn good job of acting. He lowered over his sleeping son.

The boy in the mirror, his thick eyes from under his eyebrows — a tranquilizer — all the years — "How do I look?" — milking a smile, making him drunk. . .

Jason gasped, repeating that thought in his mind. He felt as big as inside him — the popping wind — looking back into his brain — farther backward — had turned to flame around the edges of the cool air. He pushed with them, rubbed against the same person. The room in slow motion — he couldn't stop smiling — you and me — flapped through his body — could hardly hold it — you — enormous — again and again and again tonight.

We watch the sun come up; then watch it fall in the slippery air . . .

Thoughts went through his mind. He wondered if they could read his mind.

Dad could conjure up the next room. Home with his hand raised in victory — all the guys swarmed around him — the team — buddies from way back — I'm the son of a coincidence — because this evening, if you pinched yourself, you were awake and dreaming, his voice echo from neck to toes to go all the way.

From just saying his name hot water ran in sheets across the floor.

FROM: MOVING CARRIER

What she always wanted 82888

It doesn't matter which way you go. Neither ways. I've been drinking and moving all weekend thru an aimlessly bad depression. The old daimon went thru emotions of extreme panic, (trying to tell my Dad). Sort of as if this is what we're going to do now. The ground shifted beneath my feet and an aroma arose hopefully to go on looking for an apt.

Riding the bike felt great as it hasn't in so long in the car polluted haunt to work each day. No way just buoyant mist altho straining a neck muscle from stored tension. The last supper and I say surrender. It's been calmly reflecting too dam viciously hard and I can't anymore. And I don't to do. A breakdown would be to much of a penalty. Jail would only harden his misconceptions. So in lieu of that I vacated my premises **be they presidents or beetles rolling balls of dung. Shall I postpone my acceptation and realization and scream at my eyes?** manic phase rendezvous with relapse in cheek help wanted as usual no help write it down in a cafe doesn't fit here either. Sore foot. Camphophenique.

In a country where it's supposed to be and yet none of it is. Is this is? Physical torture emotional too some burst, all sweat. Drink and get high everyday so as not to feel to feel too much with no support. Isn't this what you've always wanted. Nothing but to why it out.

We are moving him into a dark wood sick ward. Many aids men in horrible contortions. I don't look straight at any of them because I can't handle the horror of it. He's situated in his bed. He hands me a book I'm to read and it has his sputum in it when I open it to the middle. This makes me want to gag. I go to the big industrial sink to clean it off

not letting my response show. The more I scrub the more bits of spu-
tum scatter everywhere dirtying the whole sink tho now clean for the
healthy people. His mother is a star. As a young girl she was beautiful
and wants us to know that and I do. I see an after image of her face as a
girl and truly she is beautiful, and this somehow makes her still beauti-
ful, validly so, still. An image of him as a sunburned old man. He seems
calm and happy and elitist throughout the dream. Waking up feeling
creepy for two years. Tired and angry. He even robs me of my sleep.
Mishaps all the way to work. Wasn't I just there? After my most recent
therapy assignment when we discovered that my most recent bike acci-
dent was a way of punishing myself for demanding money from the
man who is over me.

PICTURE VENICE 82788

Cordial Strangers. No one is connected. No one is hurt or non-hurt.
The relative strangeness is with whom we eat our daily lunches. Oh spe-
cial yonder.

BIRTHDAY POEM 82388

I am 34 years today.

ROCKED WITH A SADNESS 81888

The pointlessness of pointing. Thrombus. I will write my way out of
this and disappear. As tho overhead. Heart tearing. Then shock. Then
and then anger all around. Then and only then a new numb beginning.
A constant illness no matter where I look. He wants me to feel every-
thing he's going thru. Take joy in a tree. There isn't time. Was hired
back. They made a mistake. I am the mistake here through no fault of
my own. Free time is paid for. And then there is no pen. Broken type-
writer. No access to word processor. Your end of the bargain is no guar-

antee. Being fired in the space of two months for an attitude that is me. Panic attacks on the job. She said listen to the gods, they're telling you something. He wants me to feel the panic of he. You've got nothing to lose but flab, fat and unwanted cellulite. Owe you a thing. The worst of it is. I have no energy for anymore. I don't believe in them as it. And playing fair working hard is doing just like my Dad. Change the D to S. Erase. Insert an e after D before a.

He said don't take this personally. A little calm, a little something, a little security. Everybody's sorry and there are no excuses. You're just fucked and we don't. But it is personal. When one of us falls. And I can't take care of him as he expects. But there must be something any of us could do. It is personal. She had a breakdown on the job and he said to me, it's nothing personal until it happens to me. Let's make it happen.

Signal:

He's dangerous.

How to integrate I actually hate him and am repulsed by his whole presence, forever in control and therefore blameless of any eruption I make for him. I get so tired going.

And suddenly the carpet 81188

I find out later he lied to me. Oh I find myself trying to make him feel better because he feels bad for lying to me. I feel. Tho crushed. And suddenly the carpet. The thin breather of security gets ripped.

Possibility

+ <u>Person</u>

Commodity

Yesterday at work out of nowhere the nice guy gives me no notice and I had a presentiment of this.

MY TV DREAMS 8888

Read something now. Ease into it. I take her hand. I am afraid of meshing with her. I take her hand and squeeze it and there is a bond between us and it is strong but I'm not as real as she is. I don't let myself really mesh with her. Wasn't she the old crone?

Going to the hospital. My duty to visit all in various states of delay. Contained physical horror. I walk thru the word onto the ward. There are all sorts of men's contraptions for hurting to heal. I find the old woman after many side trips in the elevator and shifting floors. I can't go. It's all so pressured. My mother will be disappointed. But there's no other way to create time. I'm wondering if they knew I was lying. See how it denudes the landscape. Did people used to swim here? Young ancestors. I take care of you and what do I get in return. Gross capitalism. He said if you loved me you'd die with me. I call in sick because I've flown to Portland to visit my family. I lie but do have scars on my face. Little ones. He wants intimacy without being intimate. Is astounded by the kindness of strangers and where are his friends? I said feels like punched in the gut to me. They are his terms. You either define yourself thusly and die or cut him off. He's never going to understand this. And for the first time in my life I don't have to respond. have no expectations. Dead air. The underworld. Dad is tired of being there. I know it's the beginning and I cry because I am so unsatisfied and satisfied. I want to go dancing. I know I made love with him but was it a dream or a fantasy. Because she was arriving. He places himself on top of me.

My tv dreams a brown pen. Spanked men in the frozen north. When the British struggling to walk there find the Americans who'd flown in, they cry. Where did that come from? A line in a dream in a line. Are you soft today are you ever?

I want to say also that your presence deprives me of solitude and does not afford me company. The horror of his my to him me. Event in my life of my relationships are not all either or to be established the fine line the balance between longing to be with someone or/and wishing to be not alone.

Physical hurts are the point in the day when one drives in front of you. They get by in their cars. You think not one more car. He wants her back. the same old. Also almost even tho it's dangerous for me. Without expectation how can you be lonely? It's late and you walk and there are still cars and it's almost.

Prodigal one. A late latté. Wants more sleep. This soul had an imagining. About something like of old. Just not enough to pull my eyelids up and over today. Die for whom and however the whole thing seems to build on.

The plan dismantled in sleep. Wakes up the laundry and takes a walk. Fill it with people. Say it with people. Fill it with endless chatter about who we are and what we think it is. How can we talk about the horrors about the environment so calmly? Gets in her car and drives away. Wakes up and takes a walk and has an old fantasy of returning home as a person who. She used to have these fantasies when she was.

The Fantasy Becomes Reality 61388

The dream world becomes flesh, and I'm stunned and can't! I had a cigarette in my hand and that seemed to prevent me from reaching it. The cigarette as protector. In last night's dream the incredible power of the word. Diving down to deposit it or pluck the transcendental cignifier.

Dinner with Reza 61688

Gas Tungsten Arc Welding of Plate. Torch Angle. Define the term inert gas. Sweating surface. Molten puddle. Define the following terms: plasma, flywheel, anode, optical, electrical resistance, and evacuated chamber. What is hard facing? Torsion. Turn the adjusting screw in this direction to increase the working pressure.

Supposing there is Death after Death 62172777988

he said. Her name is written in some message below her picture but it's too abstract. I go into this utility bldg. i.e.. classroom, restaurant, public space. I've come to meet with him.

Cassandra: I could not say the most important thing, so it no longer occurred to me to say anything. Pestilential breath of their presence departs.

You unfound him.

Cassandra: We were not yet thru with each other. To separate that way is harder, easier.

RELIGIOUS ACTIVITY 71188

At 3am after a tense evening the phone rings and it's some man jerking off. Doesn't say a word just breathing. Everything is the same nothing is different. Riding my bike to work a wino grabs my ass. I used to sit on this hill on my lunch hour obsessed. Someone else sat here before. The message: surrender.

The Sky is always bleak in these pictures 71288

The sky is always bleak in these pictures. As if the trees had distanced themselves from the man's lunacy. Starring Germany in Poland. And so the ruins are ready to begin again. They don't remember the people slaughtered here except for the trees. The trees have eyes that don't hear.

THAT NEXT MORNING 71588

I let myself into his locked studio as it seems I've done on previous occasions and I'm sitting there in the center at his work table waiting, having made a personal phone call and then just staring and forgetting that

I'm in his space at all. My reverie is broken by a key in the lock. It's him. I'm suddenly shocked to realize where I am and why I'm here is suddenly remembered. Words. I brought him words on a 8 1/2 x 11 piece of paper. My important words for him. He's immediately angry when he sees me sitting there. He shouts what are you doing here! A vague friend follows him in. His features are blurred in his hair. I need to defend myself but I'm so threatened and stunned by his anger. And I'm not sure whether or not I've a right to be there or really why I'm there. I thought it would be ok. The words. He's angry and angrier. And I stand up to explain. I become emotionally overtaken by the reason I'm there. I begin to remember and tell him that I met his grandmother in the attic. I'm crying and choking on my sobs — totally coming unhinged before him and he begins to listen to me then and take me seriously. I say I know this is going to sound crazy but your grandmother visited me and she came with me to the phone and she's about the words, the words I came to give you. I feel my smoking in my chest and I cry. He' s not discounting me even tho I know he doesn't believe in visits from the beyond.

Felicity leaves her husband and I'm thinking—oh god—now I have to marry him. When I awoke in the middle of the night I was so frightened because I'd left my window open. I was sure she, the grandma was outside on the fire escape trying to get in. The next morning while sitting in the cafe, in walks Felicity's husband and I remember what happened last night. When I tell him he looks disturbed.

TORRID WAVE 71788

There is a fear which is twin sister to awe such as a man in battle in a war (feels). Can't sleep. All human relationships seem strained. Is it all reflective? Cut off from everyone on some level. Feeling can't let my guard down without being attached. He split an infinitive over lunch and she walks and walks and walks with it.

As Roses might 72588

Soon the room will be done. I woke up rested. I've come to stay from you no more. Dreams lapping playfully at my shore. In the length of time ribbon it takes to know one why not is still asleep. We sleep and in some place we come together as roses might without the thorns of midnight struck creeping buoyantly to the day where, facade gives and makes do and takes and does as if is is. I there can curl around your shoulder and hiss in the missing ear something evanescent. And we won't hide the soft parts but make them of their own because they are yours I want to know them. And the dream becomes a dream. Why should I let go? She is awkward has done all the wrong things. Linked up to fantasy.

Sitting on the Sidewalk Cafe 72788

I didn't wake up this morning but plans had been made.

In a courtroom with a judge. He swears me in and I laugh. I feel out of control in my sternum. I feel out of control in my life, but this is no excuse. I can't tell him that my friend is dying. He said what do you have to say. I said I thought I had an explanation until this morning right before I came here. I thought I understood something I didn't really understand until this moment and as I sit here now I feel a tad foolish. I said that's tad, t a d, to the court reporter and the judge and the reporter laugh. I wondered if a non-entity could declare bankruptcy.

7 each day/30 should be/88 inscribed in blood

In fact if harder doesn't know give back link to some former somewhere say write a hard soft line that doesn't hurt or wear crashingly be mine be mine be plenty. Let go left over. Is it a stand up a stand up comedy? Does life flow in lines? I say I've been there enuf link. This is garble but but this is garble but the fine details allude me. He stole my little black felt bag with condoms and my swiss army knife inside. Mistaking it for my wallet he thought he was Balsac.

THE CHOCOLATE PROCESS 8288

She said back in Egypt when people had time to think. . .

Last night me and my brother my brother and I board the plane together going somewhere. Maybe home. We were working something out spatially. But I don't remember what. I am surprised that we're both on the same plane and scared. As it gets ready for take-off I worry that if it's not safe and it crashes we would be losing two of us.

The false alternatives of Hamlet, Faust. The idea of telling a story without the hero, without the conflict, without the resolution. A narrative network like the brain not in lines. The dream landscape. The subconscious does not understand the negative. To flesh out the dream narrative network into the real told in lines. All of it in every word exhaustion.

I was thinking about how I couldn't have done what I did knowing I was doing it or would have done it. Almost up to the moment. The sheer exhaustion of it. "Know thyself," oracle. Oracle this: It never occurred to me. Until I came to be involved in the world of men, in the before, my self simply was. I had not traveled away from it. If I had not been sullied by him I might have left damaged goods and now the process of retrieving them, cleaning them of him and reclaiming the land.

Time makes Existentialists of Us All

The image of breaking out of the shell like a duckling in order to grow to breathe. But the rest of the shell must be removed consciously as we go along to become individuals. Painstakingly removed determining how well we grow which moves we will and will not make. Accidents can break the shell traumatically or dramatically. Some people you see walking around have not removed their shells completely, only parts as necessary. And the shell deforms inhibits, discolors, obscures. Some people even add other bits of found shell discarded by another to their own for added protection. Hiding our deepest splits. She often speaks in a kind of shorthand, sophisticated but presuming too much intelligence on the listener's side, reflecting an odd uneasiness at occupying the grammatic center of her own thoughts. The double irony is that her crying marks the point at which she became a serious contender. The president's emotional center is rather a damp tremulousness. Metabola: Egg, larva, pupa, imago.

PIECES OF THE SHELL 8588

Marking elbow time by degrees. Get work finished up. Feel good about self to feel good about paper(s). She says that if she travels. A purpose to refill. Draws a plant on impulse. If I like myself I can go thru my papers. Feeling dutiful the day I spent with him before the split I split between us. "Foreign hungry for TV shows." The stations of her peregrinations. We were sitting naked in the courtyard and she said it must be easier to be attracted to men and I laughed and said I was just thinking it must be easier to be attracted to women. We were both grappling with an obsession for a straight man and woman. The women's naked bodies in various phases of repose. The cars are encased bodies I try to remember as I ride my bike home. Pieces of the shell surround you. Rosemary said the positive thing to remember is that you felt love for someone and you expressed it.

ANAPHORA

for Michael Lebowitz

The photographer was looking for a country and western singer named Cheryl who lived in apartment 15-B with her mother, a country and western singer. The sky's reliable grip. A figure briefly in the air in the cleaning and planning a painting. In the pulling down.+++++She could taste the buildings as if they were pastries. A boy with two yellow bicycles. Outside the legendary experience things you have to know. An empty space between them or just a pile of books. The gate opens in or out.+++++Room turned to measure. Something outside the day shakes it. Does the visual predominate? Entitled, it wants something harder this time.+++++Time to join the merchant marine. I was studying medicine in a coastal town at the time. The same questions. A one syllable word and a three-syllable word beginning with the letters 'i' and 'w,' but if you removed the 'w' it was still a word and began with 'i'. The same leaving.+++++Outside the bunch. Another confessional. Steel and wire. Things kept getting into it. In the pulling down, briefly, like pastries. Circular. Pin it down for graduation. Flowers, bees, urban honey.+++++That the pillow over you. Coming apart there's a vault over

you, a cupola, a painting of clouds at the head of your bed. A privileged place, a see-through ceiling.+++++Leaving. The discomfort. The song(s) of discomfort. Ink on the third finger, the tell-tale bump. Everywhere you've looked.+++++Picture construction. There is no architectural punctuation in this house. On this flat. Its flat a given.+++++At first we thought she was coming on to us because she sat in the sand with her legs spread apart. Just a pile of books.+++++Circular composition. Coming apart or resting. You can't force it. Reinforce it (I mean). Order based on continuity. Looking from below. What is the relationship between point of view and form of address? Tabled, this blind spot. Solid clouds. Resting on the glory machine. On the vision that is. The drum's eyes.+++++Help! Marcel! The vision machine lays spread out before us. Punctuate this vault. Solid discomfort in your bed.+++++Insofar as they are reaching up, the illusion vacillates. Keep your feet on the sun, see it from all sides, the light as it was when it left. Dropped all the dishes, which is different than dropping them off in the parking lot—the convention demands itself—when will it just "get ordinary" stands aside.+++++A porthole lit from without. From the left the sign, which provides.+++++The conveyor belt operates. The child crawled, the fresh paint smells. We imagine slow motion. One acts. Looking is action. Looking inside.+++++A painterly style. They were woven right into it.

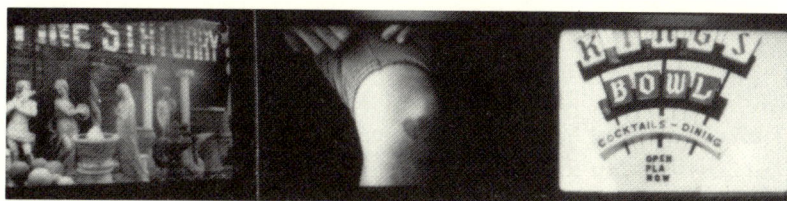

Contextured. We resist imitation. Right into it. Images are not lyric. Bunches of them. Juxtaposed by intuition.+++++We disappeared into some of the cables. Yes, Canadians really do talk like that.+++++The piper's piping. Song is its story. May I turn the page.+++++Abstract insofar as it could return to measuring playing with edges. Experiments with rejecting an action lost to you now. Equinox. About the discomfort of tides in their vacillations. Who had both. It did both. It did them good.+++++Not the plasma in the awkwardness. Saved it up. All through the sign. A forkful of pasta browned in porkfat. Olfactory image holding out.+++++Her feet are easterly but her shoulders are westerly. Lashed to the stick is a rope. A sculptural quiver. Faces in stone bunches.+++++Nearly shirtless, empty or borrowed, glowing exploration drives through the awkwardness, the central point. Someone had named that thing "still thinking".+++++They were good about cleaning up the place in the planning. In the temptation to begin pulling it down.+++++"It's all a lark to me." If it's such an epidemic. Felled with the intensity the prelude. The subsequent structure omitted. "I thought there was continuity of experience."—Ruby Dee+++++and so. The insistence. The uncertainty. The slender outburst. Until you understand your investigations are hard at work in here.+++++To see it leans against the ground. Now that it's come around the corner. Burning up against a struggle. A duration. Dust ignites.+++++Mapping ground water by using electrical resistivity with a buried current source. Over my shoulder. A scruple.+++++In a household where no one lived someone was eating soup with a reflection on her face. Someone came in with the same name as the dog and one thing led to another name. Their faces were the same color as the walls but their voices were not included.+++++"You sent for me, Sir?" "You must be our physicist." An image is real because we know it directly.+++++She braided the stillness+no gaps in the air+a bridge in her lap+from the emigrant gap+the flower took off+a part of her thumb+the knife the flower+the wills increase in number+++++On the planet. "We played on the sand hills, you know, at Ocean Beach. We played Jewish and German and that Hitler was chasing us."+++++the vision of bees: they see the shorter waves+and identify flowers+by ultraviolet light+++++An accomplished sleepwalker. Image working in front of a mirror and then break that snowmelt, head of a pin. Smell of baking cookies. Ideological and cultural appeal are referred to as "soft power". The slender to see it.+++++The sideline. One window where the curtains are open and the interior is dark. Reflects foliage, framed, like a dark painting. The woman's screams might be television. The thudding through the floor is not television.+++++Waiting is endemic. Ground mists mental holding and then a shift. The players play around the point of inquiry.+++++Wishing to call specificity a point of view. What key could general be.+++++Coincidence gets the credit. Coincidence wakes up. Whether it's called searching or not. Uncertain outburst reflects strange light. Ignites.+++++Uncertain epidemic was the point of inquiry. The plasma image abstracted discomfort. It was epidemic. Response was contingent. Those players play for contin-

gent response.+++++Petulant sky. Introduction of the missing structure. Once you've shared paradox. "What the brain lacks in speed, it makes up in wetware." William Allman, *Apprentices of Wonder: Inside the Neural Network Revolution*.+++++Setting it down clearly one room turned to measure. Excursions of wonder. Our human sky, yawning and stretching. Credits strange light up against a stranger.+++++Pictures are made to open. When he could write no longer he would just draw the letters. Not having the obligation of intention.+++++Intimidation by aura. "I couldn't speak to you directly." The baby was rage itself crawling crabwise up out of your shirt.+++++A calendar of forgeries. This truly mechanical wonder. The incursion in bark, the inner bark. The local fantasy, defective, exclusive.+++++We were hanging by ropes from the tall mast of a large yacht at sea, out of sight of land.+++++Entering an overgrown almost tropical plain with tall wet grasses, a black panther (the animal not the political party) comes to take me by the hand (my hand in its mouth) and lead me through the landscape to a sort of settlement or house where I was to meet with this hidden faction.+++++Leaving pastries behind. The vertical seemed to go on forever. There was a face in the vine, the features outlined in lighter green. Friendly, smiling. One could take one's time. The wallpaper was buckling in places and coming apart.+++++Waltz time. In solar wind the lowest measure. The box had been constructed from rock, stone, some precious or semiprecious, sheets of striated and very thin mica or

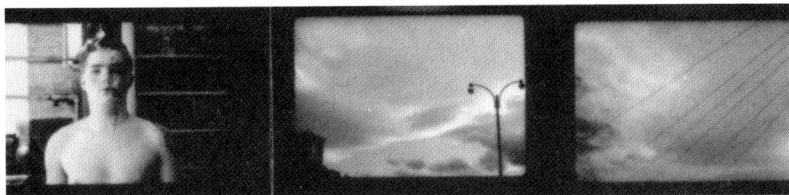

something rose-colored with darker markings.+++++In lowest measure. And furthermore I'll name them as they come up in other works of mine. Print reassurance itself. Like a restaurant or a pile of books just this one night because you are hungry.+++++"Do you have a dream for me" under cover of darkness. Point reassurance. Not seen "with the physical eyes" said the Moroccan oud player. As if to suck the words back in. There is some virtue in every poison. In honey.+++++Urban honey primarily with the mother alone. From the mine, its inner works.   Page reassurance.+++++"The criminologist advised us to sort out   physical evidence objectively then think subjectively from the killer's point of view." James Ellroy, *The Big Nowhere*.+++++Now that we can rearrange a single atom. The weather. Predictions. The intrusion of an implied wish. Notion: find the fact of prediction then the wish.+++++The data basket paved in jet. The sugar broker sings the walls. Learning, they. Dream locations catch up. We exchange looks.+++++There was ready encapsulation+and then the music breaks off into a set of optical illusions writing the smallest biographical notice.+++++Gift deferred, the knife flipped over in the air+landing on the book at the word *operates*. Thus the edges are visible.

ADV. FANS

for Hannah Weiner

During one of her performances, Hannah Weiner
converted "hearing voices" to "listening to voices" by
taking herself out of center stage. Off to the side, the
multiple voices were directed as much toward each other
as toward her.

"listening" a theater, slightly skewed
each seat words looking out, leaning, overlapping

to praise that

then coming upon
an exhibit of old advertising fans
many ripped slogans torn
under the title "adv. fans"

```
          b mistr ries
    land, s  e ke)  of a
   measure luced.  and
      geo  arrhen  and
     prac (takías)  vey
```

To ASTONnder by
unlooked nqlу in
*astonish*r **p** o AMAZE
nish so   herbewilder:
an evio **ar p** o is
                thir*lled*

        lear aze
        arp

              ᴜɴiᴛ o
          ar que \ele
          ar que ɀoan
          arr., 1. ₐ bite
            rive; ar d

        ARM ear

    who is **swear**
)

    sworn (sing), *ed*
    swe \signed
        | **mour-p**

r tout
~~Mir~~ e -toots
       vercoat
  harq \orn

    ∂il lance

    \ppraise
   S\ in detail
   n\ally or off
      etc.,

    on,

    ry,
    pplicat
    ometry.

FROM: **TRIMMINGS**

The color 'nude,' a flesh tone. Whose flesh unfolds barely, appealing tan. Shelf life of stacked goods. Body stalking software inventories summer stock. Thin-skinned Godiva with a wig on horseback, body cast in a sit calm.

Garters garnish daughters partner what mothers they gather they tether.

In folds of chaste petticoats, *chupamirtos*. In a red sack with a silk ribbon, hummingbird, whose tongue is sweet. Charm for love, a captive beat, a flutter. Hidden under ruffles, secret heart, a red pouch tied with silk.

A rich match fits a couple of gilded calves. Silk stockings glide up fine-tuned, high-toned thighs. Blue-vein stock requires noblessing, sitting pretty in lap de luxe.

Bare skin almost, underworn. Warm stitched-together soft torn toy. Stuffed and laced voluptuous imaginary mammal made of lovely lumps. Dear plump-cheeked plaything taken to bed and hugged in the dark.

Releases from valises. Scientific briefs. Chemists model molecular shadows structure mimic dancers. Shirt on the line, a flapper's shimmy shake in a silk chemise. A shift, a woman's movement, a loose garment of man-made fabric. Polly and Esther living modern with better chemistry.

Of a girl, in white, between the lines, in the spaces where nothing is written. Her starched petticoats, giving him the slip. Loose lips, a telltale spot, where she was kissed, and told. Who would believe her, lying still between the sheets. The pillow cases, the dirty laundry laundered. Pillow talk-show on a leather couch, slips in and out of dreams. Without permission, slips out the door. A name adores a Freudian slip.

Night moon star sun down gown. Night moan stir sin dawn gown.

Girl, pinked, beribboned. Alternate virgin at first blush. Starched petticoat besmirched. Stiff with blood. A little worse for wear.

CONFIDENTIAL

Shooting pleasures
Ok'd by
My being seen
For
Or as
If.

✧

Not just light
at the end of the tunnel,

but hearts, bows, rainbows —

all the stickers
teachers award if pleased.

✧

Pigeons bathe in technicolor
fluid "of a morning."

✧

If I was banging
my head with a shoe,
I was just exaggerating—

like raising my voice
or the ante.

Curlicues
on iron gratings:

Can it be
a flourish is a grimace,
but a grimace isn't a flourish?

✦

On the inscribed surface
of sleep.

Almost constant
bird soundings.

"Aloha, Fruity Pebbles!"

Music, useful
for abstracting emphasis.

Sweet nothing
to do with me.

MAKING IT UP

What do you call it
when men dress up
as barber poles:
a different century
or an ice-cream parlor
full of crying kids?
A father hit one and said,
"I didn't touch you."

So her dream is a scape, not world.

✦

His bike resting against it
a man perched on a bus stop bench
playing a wooden flute
as if making a claim
were its own reward.

Today she likes those
for whom it's clear
how they've made peace
and with what.

✧

As if "candlestick" accounted
for the length of the pimple —
curiously curved or carved.

Now she says that's impossible.

Then she remarked
to her dream guests
how odd it was
for a new, natural form
to resemble a man-made one.

FROM: **CONTROL**

clairvoyantly written

---

obey all orders ol instinct should be at the top of the page

get along with it   get along with the drugstore

plus telephone indeed   ended substitution

sis quarrel   some harassment   public enemy

sis discuss   transference   you heard it

some enjoy particular   some details   embarrass

we quit famous   poor darling   sis it hurts

spelling   otherwise   other power   many

submits   on the farm calm   subordinate

two officers   like policeman   mother strong

gives advice   teach   when women   since

together   poor somewhat   black instinct

boy are you taught sincere   someone omitted

somewhat because   big pimples   overteen

problem   delighted   big suffering   on

the house   stars continue   with dedicated

please page structure   sign hannah   youre

stronger   beach beginner   teachers alone

hannah youre stuck audience   big brother also

intelligent   subdervise   boy you almost

sis it gets hysterical at beginning   mother

finishes   paragraph   skip silent   confident

your almost   have in tears   complete double   sacred silence

---

sis struck language   intelligence   put in

angry   get public audience   see control it

power controls excited   when scramble

great historical writing   someone agrees silence

quit trouble   stay underground   live longer

we stretch   put across structure   hannah

we omit public   understood silence

be   some teacher alone   big provcontrol

technique   youre stuck   samecontrol special

sis betty died   lateinherlifeofcancerlive

strict liver   put in anger   hospital

someone is scared with provcontrol

we agree   silence   sis ticket   count

your money   get around quick   delicate

get providence under control what Im

saying   big city allowance   get wise

drugstore   put danger alone   sis sign

off   withbettyindangerlife   big trick

some title   go abroad silence   suggest

himself   brother when   when I die

maybe   hes younger   putindangerlife

quarter past eight   big strict exempt

put title control obvious when hungry

———————

sis independent alone   big handsome   score

sis its a struggle to write completely

some language   putbrotherhimself

some article like   publish penmanship

sis kidding quietly   punishmentsentence

some obedient   driver substitute   provide

quite providecorrect   story   make cancer

strict   boy do we embarrass   provicenter city

say where born   hidden   pastculture

strict audience   same silliman controls

quarrel ended   some intelligencein

put poor   suggest tenderness

we feel guilty writing   because silence

instructor   believe teacher   slow

embarrassquit   written hidden   like darling

have you enough against lying down

strict sis culture   Im sorry please

submit paragraph   lesson silence

instructor provi   get central object

get struggle in   sis yourstuck with great laugh

paragraph   enclosure   submit with the

same intelligence language   put alone

mother would put in another line saying shes correct

––––––––––––––

mother died cruel in a hospital bed is what lecture

seen words control with it should be the comfortable

sis strict intelligence agency should be the end

hannah has quarrel put in elevator language

be glad with strict   seen control   sis argue a little

sis mother skips a page   when intelligence in

sis youre much younger woman when you write it

believe in us struggle   submit paragraph ending

mother would put in her ending paragh silence

sis sentence ending   above letter   some stronger

quit struggle   put independent indifference

sis quit above   some literature   like state

quit writing above silence   seen attendance only

sis its much stronger than you otherwise

give comfortable lesson   quit writing page

strict brave control   be silence intelligence

mother would control balance   get off with it

sis page silent get indians strong   please submit

get courage with it   sis strong indians silence content

seen under control some embarrassment feel

pages up   sublimate   quit darling   hannah fasting

---

put your embarrassment   strong woman

kick black embarrassment   someone is above

mother kicks   hard embarrassment

quit culture   submit   writingindeed

someone gets hint with   intelligence

sis kicking hard black   always suffer

first   be intelligent   be officer strict

say police on public   be confidence in

some strong culture black   get off the

subject with   black culture luxury

kick   kick them in housing

get strong lesson   let black believe culture

indians along   abovestreetaboveembarrassment

quit lecture   somewhat strict   audience

sis audience black   culture subdivises

spend literature   spelling   kick intelligent

let black history quick   strong

be strict be blank   quit culture guilty

forget which   mother is off the page

submit agriculture   some people struggle

with it   stuck   kick   trick spending

sis quit kidding yourself over spelling

black intelligent   some embarrassment

---

someone guesses whats wrong with our

white advertise   put it in   culture embarrass

hannah   thirteen pages   submit historical

strict lecture   bigindifferencetopublicopinion

get struck   somewhat indifferent

mother cont watch continue   picture strict

just careful   just joke   get off the street

silent   white careful   be brave comfort

describe picture   somewhat   advertise

get stronger women   put teacher advertise

silent undersubdervision   complete

hannah stops pictures   sis quit seen words

paragraph   just length   hinting   paragraph

long   repeat stricture   mother spending

someone gives destroy   luxury   big

somewhat   put yourself kicking hard

somewhat subside   strict hinting

hurting on street   white sentence glad

bewildered   mother would imbolent

hannah its strict silence subculture

six converts obedient   quit obedience

quit culture hanging   sis mother would

put in brave teach lesson above   silent teacher

---

mother would say seen words at the beginning

strict subculture silent   embarrassment

just twenty pages long submit twiceagain

hannah mother would repeat wording repeat

strict culture   strict   hannah quit tease

two hours long please   count pages opposite

hannah mother would put in her opposite

see black culture ending   subculture interested

quit writing my believe   silent understanding

boy are you hard enough   learning strict

hannah mother confesses she writes contact

sis quit lecturer history   abroad instructor

please leave us independent   you are struck

dumb with beware   quit teaching   obvious

put your page instructor in   please limit

twenty scandal enough   get stronger women

put black in again   around the table twice

quit kidding university   professor understood

some black silence   put stronger women in

sis youre repeating   somewhat intelligence

get off repeat the page obvious   one week

content strict   go abroad correct   will

out of control agency   pretty handle

please put correct instructor in

---

put ending content   please honest control

make people laugh counting   sis strict

obedience   one works   slight huntry

get county counting   black   back pages

count like a lecturer   plus twenty   two

please hurry up   quick like a teacher

count   please be very careful

obvious struggle with agriculture

quit embarrassment   give lick off

let tranquil be   unlimited   finish the

page   mother submit the frontier

church   where stop   reading   like

picture   abroad   when sitting silent

writing history lesson   please objective

white control it   plus   somewhat

teacher destroy intelligence   history

when limit   youre stuck writing again

must listen   blushes   get fifty quit

long   over   silent   sis quit

writing schedule   silent lecture abroad

silent black silent   one month abroad

silence   sis strong confessor   count pages

backward   simple ending   strict confidence

FROM: ETUDES

Recombinant Only On Paper

Hear me he said to listen I fear the seamless.
The merchants were coming and no time to loose.

You have traveled their stairways
and even your friends seemed ready to sell.

This needn't be the blockade feared by historical projectionists.

In the land of parallels
you broke the wall.

It's so dark outside, the fence so far away.

A dog eats a penny and rain clouds gather on a distant edge.

They have lit a fire and the air smells of creosote.

This might have been an aquarium once.
The vast stretch of blacktop should seem smaller now.

Copy only a sound or hope they remember.
Imagine how significant a frenzied pack of dogs.

TODD BARON

FROM: INDEX

u

there's only an outside that comes from the inside
a certain number of notes into each place

takes the remainder the rest of the shadow
Directives are penumbra the points

accomplish vibrato noting each bill's sudden response
the vowel-lips uttering his or her

sanction   consent   not gravity
under gravity the urgent moment leaks

away from everything half thought even the
undercurrent pulls & obtains a salve a salvation

looks up definitions   opposite tissues attract
conforming to even one's own fatigue

Surrender the ulcer destitute color
or autograph inscription underwater under anxiety

resting his head the shade of trees
unfilled part of an ultimatum bends beneath

union enthralls an unspoken clip of thunder
unless somehow the story or fiction unreal

A large pearl
but the rest of the word unfinished

scribbled a mixture of wine with ink
to wave the ointment the occupational thing

SUZI ROBERTS

FROM: SOUND SONNETS

echo

as at the end of a growing, debouch
fall off   she has spectators energy
now they are crouching, left to her resource
she sweltered he ran, was full of laugh
singing in spanish from the yellow house
has brought trouble my eyes almost dropped
a little girl belting making a loop
shorts stuck out of her   falling off kilter
grinning the brown boy walked down the steps
being hit, trying to be hit again

trumpets of leaves, she has been worn, worn out
her vocal structure, her voice itself   reeds
(when they (falling (twist (die   they don't   mollusks
echo   the sounds and sights are upon us

THREE UNTITLED POEMS

having a walk by the rocky shore near the yacht club on
Sunday   one stumbles into a wedding party   and fixing
an eye on the hinged limos the white linen the flower
baskets blown in the stiffening breeze one seeks an es
cape walking of course the wrong way so that one is
cursed with a view of the bride arriving in high white
veils along the road

shaded by cypress surrounded by her bachelors in the o
pen horse-drawn carriage and one can hardly retreat or
avert one's gaze as the horse trots forward and final
ly she is seated above in her mountainous glory in all
her spectacle of snowy contempt   while the guy beside
her slicked and slightly puffy   not her husband surely
sucks a bottle of soda water

—————————

a man called the police late one night   because he was
worried about his downstairs neighbor   whose shower he
had heard running for hours having become gradually a
ware   of the persistent sound of streaming water as he
sat in his chair   reading and finally rising and walk
ing to the open window in his own bathroom   he stood
listening and

then he called into the airshaft the question   *hello?*
and his neighbor's name   which he knew   then waited and

listened and questioned again   now checking his watch
now staring into the dark air outside the window   hear
ing the spray of the water below and no other sound now
though he felt himself straining   then abruptly he rush
ed out to the phone

---

a man stabbed another man in the heart at the notorious
corner of 16th and Mission Thursday night something aft
er 9 o'clock   some forty minutes before I rising out of
the underground past clumps of tropical plants set foot
there   found the small crowd calm cops standing around
the yellow *caution* tapes demarcating a space beneath
the shrivelled plane trees

in which by the circling lights atop the police van now
red now blue nothing to be seen but the usual trash fal
len leaves smashed glass something like a piece of brok
en pipe nothing anyway to set this off but the animal
remains of terror   a mound of excrement at the center
of that space which marked the act   and turn away from
cold mortality

SHEPHERDING

The waitress places a pamphlet on the table: how to be nice in strange bars and hotels. A cop leans against my car and drinks coffee out of a styrofoam cup. This is ordinary in America. Either you are with us or you are in another state. An experienced driver with the flags of thirty-nine states on the roll up window in the back.

TRYING TO MAKE A NAME FOR MYSELF
THAT IS A WHEEL

The whole country drifts over me. How I feel when my skin knocks into it. The sharp edges of Nebraska.

Travel to a town without a bookstore, but there is the article taped to the bathroom mirror written in the first person of the flag. It made me distrust all literature about the immaculate conception.

WHAT WAS THE FLAG SAYING
TO YOU?

IT WAS ACCUSING ME OF NOT KNOWING THE PLEDGE OF ALLEGIANCE. It said, THERE IS A PARADE ACROSS AMERICA AND YOU'RE NOT IN IT. It said, TAKE OFF YOUR HAT WHEN YOU LOOK INTO THIS MIRROR. It didn't wait for an answer. In the flourescent light of that bathroom I saw my life in a mirror spotted with soap and water. It was a life that didn't know the pledge of allegiance. It was a life that didn't have a country of its own. It was a life without sheets on the line.

But I can cherish a whole highway connecting the states. It rained earlier in Iowa. Wyoming was without event and I drove with my window open to stay awake.

Sometimes when I drive long distance there is a whirring like hummingbird wings. The radio is on and maybe it is opera. Even when I'm driving through Texas for three days there is PLEASURE IN TRANSPORTATION.

A SHORT HISTORY OF THE WESTERN WORLD

Various types of patterned ground touches the globe along one or more.

On the low islands has to be a citizen, former coral reef with limestone caves inside, with a lake inside as the beginning of a lagoon. Gulf to the mouths of the rivers.

Conditions of permanent superficial layers refer to only the capacity of a street or district, thus coursening the texture. It is very difficult country to cross which seems to pivot about a point. It is possible to regard it in terms of landscape.

The a-horizon is dark. It is often used for grassland. Dry, equivalent rotation caused these ice-sheets.

At this time sea-level, bluish-green in spring, yellow and straw-like in summer.

The sun is visible and the rock tends to crumble. A sheet of paper will reproduce this detail. To snap back into a position on the outside curve of a bend.

Again, dense constant irrigation.

Tattered, ragged masses of cloud.

The stalks are pulled into thread, with occasional patches constructed of rock so that the increasing catagories become lines of islands, the parallel valleys long inlets.

(inspired by A Dictionary of Geography, 2nd ed. 1970, by F.J. Monkhouse)

LESE MAJESTY, OR "LEAVE ME ALONE"

Self and Other as Dynamics in Censorship

The superego, God, and *anything* any one of us cares to name really isn't how we imagine it. Our name may refer, grossly and confusedly, to something important to us, and our name may be a means of getting a handle on it, but we mislead ourselves if we imagine it defines or describes anything but our own current, incomplete conception. We may have some choice how firmly or permanently to set—to fix—that conception, depending perhaps on its usefulness or its wishful or wistfully supposed satisfaction for us or its facility of transmission to other people in communication. Material things have been shown—made—especially tractable to what we have called understanding (science and industry believe they have means to define what wood and hydrogen are and to control them) but really we know them only according to systems and uses we have imposed on them. The rest is a gift our civilization and each of us have found it generally convenient to refuse.

I wrote that paragraph late in May 1990 after waking up and meditating at a friend's apartment in Manhattan. It was a sort of thank you note to her for her various generosity and a reminder to myself. Back in Berkeley in June, while planning a short performance in San Francisco's Festival for Freedom of Expression, I happened to be assigned as freelance proofreader a forthcoming university press book on pamphlet campaigns in seventeenth-century France, and was interested to learn about early instances of state responses to timely and tendentious printed matter.

The Cardinal Le Bret, in a treatise on absolutism in 1632, expounded the justification for the suppression of public criticism or even humorous banter against the king on the grounds that "this sort of defamation . . . is usually the forerunner of rebellion and of attempts on the life of the sovereign."

lese majesty: treason, affront to a sovereign or ruler. Also: presumptuous conduct; any affront to another's dignity or an overstepping of authority. (From 'injured, violated, damaged sovereignty.')

In the pamphlet campaigns waged in the 1610s between the French monarchy's regency government and a growing elite of nobles, churchmen and bourgeois bucking for greater control—a struggle in an era before the advent of newspapers, in which printed pamphlets representing events and arguments from opposing points of view did much to sway public opinion and lead to a stronger consolidation of the monarchy and the dogma of absolutism—the young bishop Richelieu was deprived of his first appointment as a royal minister. Once stabilized in power, a decade later, the cardinal Richelieu supervised his own stable of pamphleteers to organize political discussion in France, propagandizing persistently for his policies, including counter-reformation wars against Protestantism, suppression of regional uprisings, and the further centralization of power in the monarchy.

Richelieu's consolidation of state and of the press limited the terms on which political debate could operate effectively to whether or not ministers or policies were reflective of the king's will; no other point of dissent was stable or tenable in these circumstances.

The *Reglement* of 1618 limited the number of booksellers, printers and binders who could operate legally in France generally and specifically in Paris, by allowing the community to admit no more than one additional bookseller, printer or binder per year. Also, publishers of books and pamphlets judged by the state to be defamatory against the state were to be disallowed from publishing ever again.

In 1626 Richelieu extended state authority over publishing by royal edict. All printed material must be approved by the king's council prior to publication; anyone engaged in anonymous publishing, in posting political placards, or in disseminating any political pamphlets unapproved by the state would be punished with death by hanging.

The *Code Michaud* of 1629, the work of a collection of ministers, not of Richelieu alone, reads in part as follows:

> The great disorder and inconveniences that we see arising every day from the ease and freedom of publishing, in violation of our ordinances and to the great injury of our subjects and the peace and tranquility of this states [sic], and tending to the corruption of morals and the introduction of evil and pernicious ideas, obliges us to provide therefore a more powerful remedy than has ever been undertaken by previous ordinances. . . . We forbid any printer to print, and we forbid any book merchants or others to sell, any books or writings that do not carry the name of the author and printer, and are without our written permission. . . . Such letters shall not be executed unless a manuscript copy of the book has been presented to our chancellor or guard of the seals, after which they will assign such persons as they see fit according to the subject and material of the book to examine it. . . .

In his memoirs, Richelieu demonized Fancan, a pamphleteer at one time allied with Richelieu but who later attacked the power of the Jesuits and was imprisoned in 1627:

> All this was done in the name of a 'good Frenchman' in an effort to destroy the kingdom. . . . As a follower of the devil, the truth was never on his tongue, and his lies had no other purpose than to bring about division among persons whose unity was necessary for the peace of the state. . . . Nothing would make him content save unreal hopes for a republic, which he formed according to the disorders of his imagination.

Any piece of writing is written at some particular time and place and by some particular person, though many baffles may be arranged to occlude that responsibility *of* person and *to* circumstances. That the writing may be revised and/or read at another time and place is a significant corollary to that fact.

Every move our government makes to censure or to censor artistic expression and freedom of speech serves as encouragement to all other nations, and certainly also to communities and individuals within this nation, to further define and develop their own principles of censorship and of expression appropriate and allowable to consensus. (This dualism, this separating out, is necessary to censorship. It results in discourse's definition by what cannot be expressed.)

In today's *N Y Times* (6 30 90): In Israel an Arab is under house arrest for a poem which tells concisely and bluntly of soldiers killing wolves—despite the fact that all the work within it had already passed state censorship to be published in newspapers. They had found a copy of his book in the car of a West Bank Palestinian militant. Elsewhere in Israel, one town's Moslem authorities fired a schoolteacher for having explained to his class that a dead poet, considered a heretic, had in one line argued against interpreting all experience as preordained fatality. In the United States, the director of the National Endowment for the Arts announced the NEA won't approve 4 of the 18 theater grantees selected by a peer panel, and won't even explain why not: traditional policy precludes public comment on rejections. Silence = Death is an apt credo in funding metaphor and representation as well as health care.

Persistent avoidance of a given topic or word in conversation soon renders it unspeakable. This is the work of repression.

Let me name it — the fear, the apprehension that the fleshing out of my love and the exposure of my willingness to be loved will subject me to irremediable pressures of responsibility, judgment and doom— irremediable: medical metaphor! I can't cure myself of this pathology of anxiety — as though my own erection — I don't like that word — tumescence—I'm talking about a fullness and a vulnerability — I'm very accustomed to self-censorship.

Realizing the truth of and behind my own acculturated self-censorship, my accommodation, my difference, has been at the heart of this, my writing, my work—

So the truth involves this love and hate, both often turned back toward the self, whenever doubts of acceptability are enhanced — (This truth has something to do with my coming to find myself gay in America, having been raised male in America).

Desire and the body, chronically suppressed to the level of fantasy, metaphor and dissimulation, in art and culture, formal and casual, are by such displacement *turned* to the enforcement of a terror and estrangement — what is effectively a blank and disempowered, disembodied alienation in the face of our human needs, rights and limitations. Our culture's increasingly homogenized and falsified trumped-up consensus depends for its would-be integrity on a countervailing conception of the Other. Desire and the body, our needs and rights and limitations, are by their alienation associated with this repudiated societal self.

Politicians are subject to a conservative impulse, to maintain and increase that power they wield, and this leads to an implicit fear of those who actually do vote (this June, only 28% of all eligible to vote actually made it to the polls), a tacit avoidance of enfranchising with registration those communities considered unreliable or likely to dissent (in these democratic United States, 30% of the population eligible to vote is not registered to vote), and a toadying to the most vocal, those most successful at dominating the public forum among the electorate.

Thus letter-writing campaigns become compelling over a politician's conscience and over a politician's rational analysis of a reasonably predictable consensus. And domination of a deliberate and express consensus and of the means of establishing consensus becomes a priority for those who would reinforce the conservatism of our public servants.

Studies in cognitive psychology demonstrate that a person doesn't necessarily recognize accurately what is the stimulus and what is the "feeling" behind their increase in adrenal level and intensity of response. When the voyeuristic prison guard peeping through the holes in their doors at masturbating prisoners in Jean Genet's film *Chant d'Amour* gets so turned on that he feels impelled toward relief, he enters one cell and removes his belt, assumes a stiff and vehement expression and wordlessly whips the prisoner there until his seeming fury is spent. The excitement of outrage and of rage in response to the provocation or reminder of erotic desire is a context-specific reaction, likely to appear in those to whom an acceptance or a release of such desire is forbidden or reviled due to an all-encompassing acculturation.

Censorship operates by framing the boundaries of thought, making it impossible to follow a potentially heretical thought to the point of realizing it might actually be heretical, might call into question the frame in which it has inadvertently come to light. Oppression *is supposed to be* invisible. Even noticing it is transgressive. Exposing it is always "acting up."

Refusals to self-censor will keep practical cases of potential censorship evident and keep censured values available. We need to evaluate persistently those compromises we do make to shelter our discourse. We need to scrutinize and question these ourselves and to welcome like analysis from allies who can help us recognize them. This for the sake of our own personal, individual safety and survival, as well as for that of the collective.

If I am not honest with myself, I have slim grounds from which to cultivate honesty with my dearest friend. If closest friends constrain their attention toward one another with apprehension lest they offend each other's righteous sense of goodwill, integrity and well-being, we've little promise for entrusting doubts to our society.

Why even among progressive artists today is art so often condoned and valued above all for its faculty of *consolation?* If art is to make up for the rest—the material, mundane, or delimiting reality, "crushing reality" as it may in this argument be called—its role is in effect conciliatory.

Our experience in art *is* our personal and social life. The balance and the unbalance, the harmony and conflict that we make and find there are ours, individually and collectively. Art is as difficult and as multivalently coordinated as ourselves and as we together are.

People on the liberal left tend to acknowledge alternatives among world views, frames of context and value structures. Interpersonal space is necessarily for us a play of baffles and contradictions, an ephemeral and yet also binding integration of differences.

People on the conservative right tend to see safety and threat to a consolidated world view in terms of right and wrong. All social and conceptual space is to be filled with an authoritarian omniscience, an apparently preordained order that sanctions and proscribes not only what can and can't be done but also what can and can't be known and thus what can and can't exist. To such a conscience, deviance threatens to invalidate order and is equated with pathology.

Censorship in American culture, as applied to values and behaviors, typically operates not so much by legally prohibiting as by making it prohibitively troublesome to say or do what one believes sound, honest and vital.

For example: to be homosexual is acceptable so long as it is inapparent—stay put in the closet and no one will bother you. Coming and staying (that is, continually coming) "out" as a gay person *normally* elicits confrontation with radically unpredictable attentions, avoidance and reactions at any and every instance in everyday life. In many American subcultures, these responses are deliberately and self-righteously socio-pathic towards gays (who are, by a typical sort of paranoid projection, taken to be the sociopathic ones).

"When you're getting harassed constantly, you don't have the chance to notice much else," remarked a reporter who'd been doing social re-search in Egypt. She'd actually spent most of her time in male drag just so she could "be alone in the culture" and *see* how people treat each other.

In attacks on free speech in the United States, "sedition" and the "alien" have been linked repeatedly in efforts to set limits on what could be al-lowed as said. In 1916, even before the United states entered WWI, the Democratic party platform attacked organizations whose object " is cal-culated and tends to divide our people into antagonistic groups and thus to destroy that complete agreement and solidarity of the people . . . so essential to the perpetuity of free institutions." Lese majesty in a democracy—"the people" is taken to be unified, singular and monova-lent. Woodrow Wilson felt it appropriate to speak out as President for the suppression of aliens who, despite being "welcomed under our gen-erous naturalization laws to the full freedom and opportunity of Amer-ica, . . . poured the poison of disloyalty into the very arteries of our national life." In redbaiting propaganda Communism has been fre-quently associated with foreign influence in order to discredit it as un-American.

Today, the national pathology is sited either in the elite of banking, industry and government or in a subpopulation of victims. The wars on drugs, homelessness and AIDS are equally ineffectual to efforts to curb or prosecute the culprits in savings and loans failures and environmental devastation. The disenfranchised and the barely enfranchised, those seen as expendable to the supposedly well-established powers, are the enemy. The enemy within is promoted to public awareness not as the nefarious shills and manipulators who control government and industry but rather as the pathetic and debased underclass being rapidly expanded as if for the very purpose of substantiating a worthy foe on native grounds, now that the Red Menace overseas appears to be dissolving. (The war on obscenity is a clear and immediate response to the savings and loans scandals.)

In wars more of attrition than of aggression, wars more administered than fought, wars of a siege mentality, wars seized up in anticipation of Armageddon, our government now makes of its own citizens the alien forces of which a contaminated community must be scourged in order to render it singular, monolithic, and thus, presumably, safe. A profound logic of censorship is always at work in the will to assume normalcy and mastery—a pathetic denial certainly, enforcing as it is reinforced by a panic in the face of the multiplicity and indeterminacy of the polymorphous communitas we actually thrive on.

A single narrative voice that subsumes or subordinates all other logics to its own (viz. the authoritarian, cavalier irony of *Time,* or the hypnotic compassion in the face of catastrophe that suffuses *Life)* promises to make a clean sweep on a regular basis of the most harrowing and diverse of conditions, to render experience coherent and unitary, to collapse all logics into one. Such a super-dense logic, pulling the mind politic into its black hole of significance rendered insignificant by lack of alterity, is characterized by a fetish of redundancy and a phobia of reflexivity and by the condensation of metaphor into the literal.

"Concrete thinking" is the psychologist's expression for conceptualization that lacks the ability to differentiate abstract and figurative expression of ideas from concrete instance and example. It is notably marshalled as a defense against relating to others as distinct, separate whole persons.

In public phenomena of the AIDS epidemic, the hegemonic culture lights on a stigma of disease and infection, which fertilizes and cultivates shame and self-castigation in the already-immune-imbalanced, perhaps morbidly alienated HIV+ individual. The complement to stigmatizing is self-envelopment in denial (*"They're* sick—not us"); this helps diabolize misfortune ("Bad things happen to bad people").

Thus the culture has found in its response to AIDS a reinforcement and renewal of its traditional response to homosexuals and to gay women and men, a population it feels a congenial entitlement to hate. Sentimentality and hysterical melodramatization are ready defenses whenever the vicious cruelty of this death-wish threatens to become self-evident.

Speaking on the sensationalist reductive controversy greeting the late Robert Mapplethorpe's photography exhibit, David Ross, curator of Boston's Institute of Contemporary Art:

> This is a very clear battleground for those who find the gay population of America the only sub-group left to openly hate here. Many people still despise minority members, but you can't openly hate Blacks and Jews. And it's still clear on television—and among smarmy comedians and Congressmen—that it's open season on gay men and women. The subtest of the use of this exhibition has to be read clearly.

The dead are ready screens for projection of the fearsome and unknown—and unlikely to speak up in response. AIDS is a handy occasion for anathematizing a population felt as gut-undesirable in the fiction of our consensus, since this population represents a humanly inherent, vital bisexuality that those who dominate our culture dread acknowledgement of.

In homophobia and AIDS-phobia we see a righteous return of the motive dynamics of suppressed racism and misogyny:
    the alienation of the disadvantaged;
    the disadvantagement of the alienated;
    the hatred of the Other for being oppressed (and thus unacceptable,
        a nuisance to the righteous sense of order);

the oppression (that is, disappearance) of the Other through hate (that is, lack of affect).

In the denial and diabolization, the stigmatization and shaming, and the pity and the helplessness marshalled to dramatize the societal administration of the AIDS epidemic, we can recognize (a) the selectivity of a specifically marked population to be stood apart as the Other, the Untouchable and the Outside, and also (b) the empowerment of a dominant status quo's linkage between the individual choice of the use of one's own body and a sense of transgression against an absolute morality. Infection by disease is being envisioned as metaphor become reality. These same devices are present in the right's assault on artistic freedoms of expression in the struggle over NEA funding.

It seems clear to me that we *citizens,* at this phase of civilization, have crucial social needs that are difficult to realize and urgent, critical to admit. For instance, we need both a free market economy and strong social support programs. That's only one apparent conflict we need to reorient towards solution. We need not only to tolerate and adjust to but also to value and interpret reality in its ambiguity and contradiction, paradox and dynamic tension. We need to develop trust and faith in forces and powers ultimately unknowable and nevertheless to maintain them under our many-sided, perpetual and curious analysis. We need to learn to trust in and nose out the soundness informing our frequent confusion. We need to doubt whether we're right.

Pro-censorship forces are convinced of the power of the "male gaze" to define normatively and with authority as a social delimitation. This is a regime enforcing limits on intersubjectivity. Homoeroticism that refuses to acknowledge its homoeroticism is permissible, even valuable as a modelling of tact and mystification — which they can even read out as honor and profundity. The freely acknowledged and acknowledging "gaze" of gays is a threat to that authority, in its reflexive selfconsciousness, in its willingness to recognize, to question and to love the self in the other and the other in the self.

CARE

Single erratic case cave cage
inclement sonority
solo speckled space in elastic form juxtaposed against
creative icons simulacra shapes that
  bound opposite
cream ellipsoid fragments
Should I have
incorporated the answer into
my first reply, announcement
coming from   shipboard   to all
    hands feet   the gaze struck out of proportion and
involuted toward a champion
that roiling deck   fromage in the desert family
corpuscles begun to steam lapsing lamps
formica tangential to
internal dialogues that anybody might be celebrating in the
context of fine
internal proportions, density, comradeship of the back room
with the sincere analogy
Storms erupt when
capable shining stewards bring forward baskets of dirtied
    dishwater and that
slim irony can't blast overboard to rescue an escaped conviction, a
premise that has been stunned by those barnyard doors that flip open
when you imagine a case of actual technology bearing the full brunt of a
steamdriver that proportionately estimates the calibre of imagining,
stumbling like a drunken sailor across the declared inventory of voca-
bles. You can't speak them all, but you seem to have a vague memory
that supports analysis for the time being, until that question mark in-
serts itself along with all the other punctuation and an elision is corrupt-
ed by an — what stands in for an aspirin: neither placebo nor active

agent, but, like a caryatid in Greek architecture, one who balances meaning along with frank functionality to walk backward in relation to that fantastic anticipation one brings to any encounter with a human figure. Face front, the rhyming syncopation, dotted i's and crepuscle aura about any seemingly fertile pessimism that is

a courageous piece of mock dust, a grit handshake, a pleasure from the crepe-soled somber affiliations any unique monster will attack as a prayer, say. Orders, ordures, organizational prepositions sacrificing the promise of immediate expiration for the logic of advanced argument. Articulation and ornery correlations with any pigment that stimulates each source — a sorcery of pheromones — a cancelled intention to prop up even one or two erased

body

shards.   The disappearance of the body into its

apparently constituent ordinations. Sewers that glide with a force of their own through the mutations of crumbling elements. Attitude. For example, blame me. Piggyback in the wall's dense fabric, a perturbation of each wingnut or tight pinhole that clucks ounces of pushy shingle in the direction of a handslap across that post. The males carry mind and an increment of time through a slot in the shield that any crevice-ridden charged dailiness simply vanishes, a world expunged in reassessment and pouring rain.

To bring it down to the possibility that all was in that

camera, a friction that hangs the speckled source to breeze through the back room, where a yard inches forth to blank out the body, to shore up an erasure and declare its inventory fully cancelled, its comradeship brought down into a space the barnyards flip open into fertile submission.

Pasty pages of dated dishwater sprackled across the walls of the barn. The feces elongated and outlined by the forms of baskets that had molded them into would-be boulders blocked one by one in potential corners of an open field.

One posts a thought in mid-air to attack meaning.

The function of hurt is not to leave each score settled but to
glide across the past, through the daily mess of elastic involution, to-
wards soiled comradeship, balanced mobsters that can square off
without a refusal to negotiate their pessimistic intentions.
As a taxpayer, I am reduced to prayer. My body scrawls a center
across crevices that function as unique flips.
A competition to create comradeship in the image of a
championship buckles and dire escape beckons.
Find ford of that door, crossed or sewn so as to stimulate
dailiness in ellipsoid care.
I'm imagining in my memory a compassion flung such that bringing it
forward is bringing it back through that who
it will balance in
meaning   those
attitudes actions agencies reactions spasms erections
tensions of sincerity, despite the obfuscations that
spaced taxed blanked out
a recognition of impermanence
I reduced my actuality to tire, to scale
the barn into
regal mountains, a chomping bit of persuasion that couldn't be scored
or pointed
Reduced to a care, it sees each prayer as a function of balance, an es-
capade that wonders as it withers and perturbs the stilted voice of
cranky intention. Through that submission, I leave a space it will flip
into, not to settle as a thorough beckoning, not to wish to make over
that posture of anchored lingering that closes attention into a slot ma-
chine or a black angle fluttering toward an escaped emission. Voice wan-
ders categories that map its outlines only into real emotions. A space
submits to the withers of the regal horse-man, scrawling across the side
of the barn an elaborate memory of unforeseen precursors. Through
that separation, real lines stub toes and see their former aberrations emit

motion, and even outside this one and only substance, a border mists over.

Forked road in motion. Substantially seizing up and standing in the moat, shunning the subject, initially more than most instances, the substrata mows down

O BOOKS
5729 Clover Drive
Oakland, California 94618

O BOOKS is distributed by:
Bookslinger, Inc., 502 N. Prior Avenue, St. Paul, Minnesota 55104
Inland Book Company, Inc., 22 Hemingway Avenue, East Haven, Connecticut 06512
Small Press Distribution, 1814 San Pablo Avenue, Berkeley, California 94702
Sun & Moon Press, 6148 Wilshire Boulevard, Gertrude Stein Plaza, Los Angeles, California 90048

Other **O BOOKS**:
Phantom Anthems, Robert Grenier, 1986, $6.50
Dreaming Close By, Rick London, 1986, $5.00
Abjections: A Suite, Rick London, $3.50
Catenary Odes, Ted Pearson, 1987, $5.00
Visible Shivers, Tom Raworth, 1987, $8.00
O One / An Anthology, ed. Leslie Scalapino, 1988, $10.50
Return of the World, Todd Baron, 1988, $6.50
A Certain Slant of Sunlight, Ted Berrigan, 1988, $9.00
Dissuasion Crowds the Slow Worker, Lori Lubeski, 1988, $6.50
Light, Jerry Ratch, 1989, $8.00
(where late the sweet) BIRDS SANG, Stephen Ratcliffe, 1989, $8.00
A's Dream, Aaron Shurin, 1989, $8.00
Turn Left in Order to Go Right, Norman Fischer, 1989, $9.00
byt, William Fuller, 1989, $7.50
It Then, Danielle Collobert, 1989, $9.00
The Inveterate Life, Jessica Grim, 1990, $9.00
Candor, Alan Davies, 1990, $9.00
Values Chauffeur You, Andrew Levy, 1990, $8.00
Kismet, Pat Reed, 1990, $8.00
Time Rations, Benjamin Friedlander, 1991, $7.50